WW2: A Layman's Guide

WW2: A Layman's Guide
Scott Addington

All rights reserved

ISBN-13: 978-1532775550
ISBN-10: 1532775555

©Scott Addington 2016

Cover design: Battlefield Design
www.battlefield-design.co.uk

Other books by Scott Addington:

WW1: A Layman's Guide
D-Day: A Layman's Guide
The Third Reich: A Layman's Guide
Waterloo: A Layman's Guide
The First World War Fact Book
Heroes of The Line
The Great War 100: The First World War in Infographics
Five Minute History: First World War Battles
Five Minute History: First World War Weapons

All books are available from Amazon sites worldwide

For special discounts, free gifts, news and previews of upcoming projects why not sign up to my newsletter at www.scottaddington.com

The right of Scott Addington to be identified as the author of this work has been asserted by him in accordance with the Copyright, Designs and Patents Act 1988.

All rights reserved. No part of this publication may be reproduced, stored in retrieval system, or transmitted, in any form or by any means, electronic, mechanical, photocopying, recording or otherwise, without the prior permission of the copyright owner.

Introduction

Six years and one day.

That's how long the Second World War lasted. In that time around seventy million people were killed as a direct result of the fighting. (yes you read that right). Millions more people saw their lives torn apart through pain and suffering. With eighty one countries caught in the cross-fire, the Second World War really was a global catastrophe.

Following in the style of other Layman's Guides, this book is more like a chat down the pub than a heavy historical text. I have tried to make the story flow naturally but have not overloaded the reader with mountains of detail. The chapters are sharp and to the point, perfect for dipping in and out of whenever the fancy takes you.

The course of the Second World War was littered with tales of incredible courage and bravery - the men and women that fought for freedom were incredible - this Layman's Guide is my attempt at telling their story in an engaging way that appeals to people that may not have read about the Second World War before.

I hope I have done them all justice.

SMA
March 2016

Contents

Hype and Hyperinflation: Germany, 1919–39

Blitzkrieg: Poland, September 1939

Blitzkrieg in the West: Scandinavia Surrenders, 1939-40

Case Yellow: Invasion of the Low Countries, 1940

We Shall Never Surrender! Dunkirk, 1940

Avenging Versailles: The Fall of France, 1940

Pots, Pans and Invasion Plans, 1940

Fire in the Sky: The Battle for Britain, 1940

Britain Burns: The Blitz, 1940–41

Barbaric *Barbarossa*, 1941

Zhukov Hits Back: Moscow, 1941

The Axis Expands: The Balkans, 1941
Operazione E: The Italians in Africa, 1940

Banzai Blitzkrieg: Japan, 1937

Murder, Inc: Nanking 1937–38

The Great Arsenal of Democracy: America, 1939–41

Climbing Mount Niitaka: Pearl Harbor, 1941

Dancing with the Devil: Wannsee, 1941–44

Kings of Asia: Japan Rampant, 1942

U-boats: The Battle of the Atlantic, 1941–42

Turning Points in the Pacific: Coral Sea and Midway, 1942

Sun, Sand and Semi-automatics: North Africa, 1942

The End of the Beginning: El Alamein, 1942

A Taste of Things to Come: Operation *Torch*, 1942

Not One Step Back: Stalingrad, 1942

Getting Grisly in the South Pacific: Guadalcanal, 1942–43

Cologne and Frankfurt Have Some More! The Allied Air Offensive, 1942–44

Tanktastic Kursk, 1943

Tunisia, Sicily and the Emergence of the Second Front, 1943

Armistice and Invasion: Italy, 1943

Anzio and Cassino, 1944

Operation *Longcloth*: The Chindits in Burma, 1943–44

Bleeding to Death in the East: Winter, 1943

Wolkenkuckucksheim: The Atlantic Wall, 1941–43

D-Day: 6 June 1944

Bocage: Breakout from Normandy, 1944

Blitzkrieg, Red Army-style: Operation *Bagration*, 1944

Coûte que coûte: *Valkyrie*, 1943–44

The Champagne Campaign: Operation *Dragoon* and the Liberation of France, 1944

90 Per Cent Successful: Arnhem, 1944

Vergeltungswaffe: Flying bombs, 1943–44

MacArthur Returns: Triumph in the Philippines, 1944

Bold, Brash and Bloody: The Battle of the Bulge, 1944–45

A Farce in the East: Russia Advances (again), 1944–45

Hell on Earth: Iwo Jima, 1945

Operation *Iceberg*: Okinawa, 1945

From the *Westwall* to the Elbe, 1945

Holocaust: Liberating the Camps, 1945

Finale in the West: Berlin, 1945

Suicides and Surrender: Victory in Europe, 1945

Little Boy and Fatman: The Destruction of Japan, 1945

Aftermath

Maps

References, Sources and Further Reading

Hype and Hyperinflation: Germany, 1919–39

The First World War left Germany in a state of chaos. The German Emperor, Kaiser Wilhelm II, fled to Holland and was replaced by the first democratically elected government in its history. On 11 February 1919 Friedrich Ebert, the leader of the German Social Democratic Party (*Sozialdemokratische Partei Deutschlands* – SDP), was elected as the first President of the new German Republic and he took control of a Germany that was volatile to say the least.

Post-war Germany struggled with the concept of peace in the immediate aftermath of the Armistice. The country was a political melting pot on the verge of revolution with fear and hatred ruling the streets. Everyone was blaming everyone else for the demise of their country and running battles, assassinations, riots, beatings and general civil unrest were daily occurrences.

If that wasn't enough, financially Germany was on her knees. The cost of the war had been huge and the only way Germany could have hoped to recover financially was to win, then at least she would have had the spoils of war to help pay off the debt. In the end, defeat meant German industrial production in 1919 was just 42 per cent of what it was in 1913 due to the annexation of vital industrial land by the Allies. Add to that some hefty reparations and a civil duty to look after a huge number of wounded soldiers and the low-morale of the German public is understandable.

The cumulative effect of all of this financial mismanagement was inflation. Before the war any German citizen wanting to purchase an American dollar would need to stump up four German marks, in July 1923 that same American dollar commanded 353,000 German marks and in December that number rose to an incredible 4,200,000,000,000 German marks. (That number is so big I am not sure I know the correct way to say it!)

Such hyperinflation made it almost impossible to import any kind of food or supplies from abroad and the threat of starvation for millions of people was very real. Food riots, looting and fights with farmers were commonplace. Businesses and public services such as trams and trains gradually stopped running as they could not afford to pay their workers. Slowly but surely, Germany was grinding to a halt

However a new currency – the *Rentenmark* – was introduced and linked to the price of gold. A deal was done with France and America to restructure the reparations to make them more affordable. Steadily things started to improve.

All the while, a degree of anti-Semitism bubbled away in the background. Germany had had a sinister anti-Semitic strain running through its culture for centuries. It was only since the end of the nineteenth century that Jews were actually allowed to own land and farm it. Twentieth-century Germany wasn't much better and after the war anti-Semitic feeling increased. There were strong rumours that many Jews had managed to avoid war service and some Germans even claimed that the Jews had orchestrated the humiliating Armistice.

It was against this backdrop that a thirty-year-old German Army corporal wandered into a meeting of the German Workers' Party (*Deutsche Arbeiterpartei* – DAP) that was taking place on 12 September 1919 in the Veterans' Hall of the Sterneckerbräu beer hall in Munich. At the meeting the corporal rounded on one of the speakers, a Professor Baumann, who was championing Bavarian independence from Germany and advocating an alliance with Austria, and completely destroyed his arguments. After a heated exchange, the professor left the hall with his tail well and truly between his legs.

The corporal in question was Adolf Hitler and after watching him in action Anton Drexler, the founder of the DAP, immediately asked him to join the party. Hitler accepted and joined up as member number 555; the party started their membership system at the number 500 to make it seem that they were bigger than they actually were.

Hitler began taking the stage as soon as he had joined up and it didn't take long before Hitler's gift for tub-thumping speeches was making a name for both himself and his party. Within two years Hitler was talking regularly in front of thousands of people and it was clear that he was the party's main man. In June 1921 he became party leader.

He quickly changed the name of the party to the National Socialist German Workers' Party (*Nationalsozialistische Deutsche Arbeiterpartei* – NSDAP, soon to become known as the Nazis) and instigated the party symbol of a black swastika inside a white circle on a red background. By 1922 the party had about 3,000 active members.

In 1923, with Bavaria threatening to split from Germany in a row over the cost of paying the French war reparations, Hitler saw an opportunity and instigated a coup in Munich – it ultimately failed and he ended up serving a nine-month prison sentence. When he was released, the political scene in Germany had calmed down substantially. The governing Weimar Republic was finally getting to grips with running the country properly and Germany was beginning to enjoy a period of stability and, whisper it quietly, moderate prosperity.

Under these more positive conditions the requirement for a noisy, aggressive, anti-establishment party such as the NSDAP was limited and over the next couple of years Hitler and the Nazis struggled to make their voices heard. Party membership grew steadily to 108,000 members by 1928 but in the elections of that year the NSDAP managed to win just 2.6 per cent of the vote. If he was every going to challenge the establishment, Hitler needed a catalyst.

That catalyst came on 24 October 1929 when the New York stock market crashed and sent the world into financial meltdown. Immediately American bankers were knocking rather loudly on the door of the Weimar Republic demanding that the money they had been lending them over the past few years be paid back. Now.

For German industry this was an utter disaster. Very quickly Germany's factories could no longer afford to keep their machines turning and German banks started to collapse left, right and centre. Organisations throughout Germany went bankrupt and workers were laid off in their millions. It was just six years after the problems of hyperinflation, but yet again almost every German family was hit with acute financial uncertainty.

In these harsh conditions it was no wonder that many Germans, who saw no real solution to their problems, started to listen to the more extreme political parties, such as the Nazis and the Communists. The membership numbers of the Communist Party in Germany almost trebled between 1929 and 1932, and to many ordinary Germans the threat of a Communist revolution was very real. This obviously played into the hands of right-wing parties such as the Nazis who promised to rid the country of the evil Communists and protect the interest of the average German citizen.

In the general elections of 1930 the NSDAP gained 6.5 million votes. They were now the second largest political party in Germany.

During the early 1930s the German parliament, which convened in Berlin's Reichstag, was in a real mess. The Nazis and the Communists fought like the proverbial cat and dog with the chancellor – Heinrich Brüning from the Catholic Centre Party – caught in the middle. His position became untenable and he resigned in 1932. In the subsequent elections the Nazi propaganda machine went into overdrive and the party won 37.4 per cent of the vote, making them the largest party in the country although they didn't have the clear majority needed for Hitler to take power.

Not surprisingly Hitler marched straight into the office of President Hindenburg and demanded to be declared chancellor. The president politely declined, saying that he didn't feel comfortable handing power to a party that was intolerant, violent and lacking in discipline. The old man was a good judge of character.

Meanwhile, the Communists were starting to become more and more influential as the Nazi party suffered a slight wobble in popularity. Senior German financial leaders were getting increasingly nervous about the growing Communist influence within Germany, and even though they may not have been natural Nazi voters themselves, they would support anyone if it meant kicking out Communism. In truth they had no one else to turn to and on the morning of 30 January 1933 Adolf Hitler was proclaimed Chancellor of Germany. In August of the following year President Hindenburg passed away, Hitler asked the German people if they wanted him to work as both Chancellor and President of Germany under a new title: Der Führer.

84.6% of the German population said yes. Hitler was now master of all Germany.

Once installed into the hot seat, Hitler quickly 'removed' many of his political enemies and then turned his attention to the sorting out the economy. Huge building projects such as the autobahns (federal motorways), new public buildings, draining of marshlands and transforming brownfield sites for agricultural use had a massively positive effect on unemployment; in 1933 there were about 6 million people looking for work, by 1938 this figure had fallen to under 1 million.

All of this industrial renovation provided the perfect groundwork for Hitler's ultimate goal for Germany: re-armament.

Hitler believed that these new factories, especially the automotive ones, could easily be converted to military production at short notice and the profits from these automotive manufacturers could be re-invested into developing tanks, aero engines and running gear. He also believed that getting large numbers of German men back into work, especially manual work, would toughen them up and get them ready for the day when they would become soldiers. Despite the Treaty of Versailles forbidding the production of any kind of gun, weapon or armoured vehicle, factories all over Germany began churning out ships, rifles, ammunition, artillery and other military equipment creating tens of thousands of new jobs.

Another bee in the Nazi bonnet was the whole notion of German self-sufficiency. The Nazis didn't want Germany to be reliant on any other country for the importation of raw materials or food. As a result Hermann Göring, Hitler's right-hand man and chief of the Luftwaffe (the German air force), set up a 'Four Year Plan' to make Germany self-sufficient by 1940. The Four Year Plan contained some radical ideas such as replacing imported raw materials with synthetic products made locally and incentives for farmers who increased food production. There were some successes; by 1939 Germany was self-sufficient in bread, potatoes, sugar and wheat, but ultimately Germany needed more land to produce enough food for the population and raw materials to keep the factories busy. There was nothing else for it but to invade and plunder.

For Hitler war was the cure to all of his problems.

In 1935 the Saarland, a piece of land in south-west Germany that was given to France for fifteen years as part of the terms of the Versailles Treaty, went to the ballot boxes to decide whether to stay as part of France or return to Germany. A massive 91 per cent of those that voted favoured a return to the Fatherland.

It was a massive coup for the Third Reich and the implications for German-speaking minorities in other areas of Europe such as Czechoslovakia and Poland were obvious. The results in the Saarland also gave Hitler the confidence to publicly stick two fingers up at the Allies and the Treaty of Versailles. On 7 March 1936 a small detachment of three infantry battalions walked into the demilitarised zone of the Rhineland (a region encompassing parts of Western Germany along the Lower and Middle River Rhine). The world held its breath to see what the Allies would do in reaction to such a blatant breach of the Treaty of Versailles.

They did nothing.

Back in Berlin Hitler was lauded as a hero and as a result the Treaty of Versailles lay in tatters.

The year 1938 was a landmark one for the Nazi regime. They not only turned on the afterburners of their foreign policy with quick and decisive occupations of both Austria and Czechoslovakia, but at home in Germany they also pressed the pedal to the metal. Any army general or political minister that was known to disapprove of Hitler's direction was either 'retired' or forcibly removed from office. All the while, the Jews of Germany were getting a bit of a kicking.

Since the Nazis had gained power, the Jews had had a tough time of it. Laws were passed forbidding Jews to work in education or the public sector; these were then expanded to include people who were married to a Jew. Between 1933 and 1938 the number of registered Jewish-owned businesses fell by 75 per cent and thousands of Jewish children were banned from attending schools. The Nuremberg Laws passed in 1935 stated that it was illegal for a classified Jew to marry a German, it was also illegal for a Jew to employ German women under the age of forty-five. As a result most of the Jewish influence in German business had been eradicated – Jewish doctors, dentists, vets and chemists were all banned from practising. By 1938 the Nazi propaganda machine was in full swing and direct violence against Jews was actively encouraged within the party, culminating in *Kristallnacht* (the Night of Broken Glass) on 9 November, during which synagogues, homes and businesses were smashed and set on fire. The Nazis claimed that this was in revenge for the murder of Nazi diplomat Ernst vom Rath in Paris by a Polish Jew, but it was felt that this was simply the trigger they had been waiting for. However, the antagonism between Germany and Poland was not to be limited to fighting on Germany's streets.

Blitzkrieg: Poland, September 1939

Poland had been an 'issue' for Germany since 1919. In the Treaty of Versailles, Poland was rebuilt and given some extra land – dubbed the Polish Corridor – that not only used to be part of the German Empire but also left the region of East Prussia detached from the rest of Germany. To add injury to insult, there was the city of Danzig that was governed by the League of Nations – despite having a large German population. Hitler wanted the return of Danzig to Germany as well as free access to East Prussia, but Poland flatly refused. Hitler started to garner international support for his plans and on 22 May 1938 a 'Pact of Steel' with Italy was formally signed in Berlin. However, in the spring of 1939 both Britain and France tipped their hats to Poland, promising that they would get in the ring if Polish frontiers were violated. A promise reiterated in August 1939 when Britain declared they would fight if Poland was attacked.

Throughout the summer of 1939, the Nazis laid the groundwork for attacking Poland by distributing stories about Polish brutality towards German nationals in these sought-after areas. German refugees were trotted out in front of Third Reich newsreel cameras regularly to recount tales of hardship, suffering and woe.

Back home in Germany, Hitler promised to wipe Poland off the map.

The problem was that any kind of fight with Poland would most likely wake up the Russian bear and even Hitler knew that his army was not yet ready for a scrap with Stalin (leader of the Soviet Union). In an effort to preempt any Russian interference, Joachim von Ribbentrop (the German Foreign Minister) flew out to Moscow on 23 August to sign a non-aggression pact with Russia. The rest of the world was stunned that the Communists and the Nazis had come together to shake hands on such an agreement, but it cleared the way for Germany to 'acquire' Danzig and East Prussia by whatever means necessary, while the Russians essentially agreed to look the other way.

When the German Army crossed the Polish border in the early hours of 1 September 1939 all of this built-up frustration was channeled into a new kind of warfare.

Blitzkrieg (lightning warfare).

As hundreds of fighter planes and bombers roared across Polish skies destroying strategic targets to a tight schedule, the tanks, artillery and other motorised armour smashed their way through the country, advancing up to forty miles a day. Nothing could stop them. On top of that a million and a half men sporting the Nazi eagle followed tightly behind - connected with all the other elements of the advance via a huge network of super-advanced communication systems. It was the largest coordinated strike ever and unlike any major offensive in the history of major offensives.

The Poles battled bravely but they were woefully underprepared for the whirlwind. Within forty-eight hours the Polish air force ceased to exist as an effective fighting force and a week later the Polish infantry followed the same fate.

Two days after the start of the Blitzkrieg, France and Britain declared war on Germany in defence of Poland. On 7 September ten French infantry divisions pushed nervously five miles into German Saarland – that was about as much support as the Poles got from their two Western Allies. They had been promised that their allies would open up a second front in the west by 17 September, but it didn't materialise. Instead, on that day the Poles got another surprise present - the Russians invaded from the east. Within a matter of days Stalin had expanded the territory of Mother Russia by a handy 77,000 square miles and 11,000,000 people, including about a million Jews. Meanwhile France and Britain did precisely nothing. France was simply not ready for war and flatly refused to launch any kind of meaningful assault. Even when asked to drop a few bombs on Berlin, both the French and Britain quickly changed the subject. They didn't want the Luftwaffe to retaliate with bombing raids against their own cities.

In a matter of weeks Poland had gone the way of both Austria and Czechoslovakia and on 5 October Hitler made a triumphant entry into what was left of Warsaw.

Hitler may have won the battle against Poland, but the real victors were the Russians. Stalin had got his hands on half of Poland and had the Baltic States in a stranglehold. In doing so he had also blocked Hitler from getting access to the vast Ukrainian wheat fields and Romanian oil – both were strategic assets he craved in an effort to make Germany self-sufficient. Even the Polish oil fields were now in Russian hands.

Meanwhile back in Germany, all of the time, money and effort Hitler had poured into military expansion were beginning to take its toll on civilian life. To pay for all of the guns Hitler had virtually bankrupt his country and almost all manufacturing was given over to the military cause. As a consequence Germany's infrastructure was crumbling before its citizens' eyes and coal supply for domestic use was intermittent at best. The Gestapo (the German secret police) was reporting widespread unrest from a population that was already getting fed up with their Führer's obsession with the military.

The other problem was that the German military machine still wasn't properly ready for a full-on European war. The Polish campaign, for all its devastating speed and lightning strikes by air and ground, showed that the German Army was vitally short of guns and vehicles of all sizes and descriptions. When Hitler expressed his wish to commence proceedings in the West, his army generals strongly opposed. They wanted time to strengthen; there was also the question of the weather which had turned for the worse. Despite Hitler becoming furious at the prospect of a delay, they managed to convince him to postpone until the spring.

When Blitzkrieg did arrive in the west in early 1940, it wasn't in France as one would have expected. It was in Scandinavia.

Blitzkrieg in the West: Scandinavia Surrenders, 1939-40

Soon after the dust in Poland had settled, Stalin invaded Finland. On the morning of 30 November 1939 twenty-six Soviet divisions – almost half a million men – flung themselves against the tiny-in-comparison Finnish force of 130,000. As the Russian Red Army commenced its march, a thousand Soviet aircraft tore into enemy territory and quickly started to smash the feeble Finnish air defense system. It seemed to everyone watching from afar that this would not be a fair fight and that Finland would not last long. Indeed, the Russians were so confident of a quick victory that they had sent their men to war in summer uniforms, despite it being the end of November.

A massive air raid on Helsinki on the first day of the invasion caused huge damage and sixty-one civilian casualties. However, instead of breaking Finnish resistance, the Finns clenched their teeth and began to fight back. On 1 December a new Finnish government was established. The People's Government of Finland was in reality Russia's puppet and in their official declaration, stated that:

'... the Finnish people receive with enthusiasm the brave and unbeatable Red Army and greet them in knowledge that the Red Army will arrive in Finland not as conqueror, but as liberator and friend.'

Unfortunately, this message didn't get through to the Finnish military who were desperately trying to defend their country's borders. Finnish resistance was formidable. Moving quickly on skis and bicycles through the thick forests they caused havoc, especially with their improvised grenades made up of bottles filled with petrol and a lit piece of rag stuffed in the neck. These bombs were quickly dubbed the 'Molotov Cocktail' and were very effective at stopping Soviet tanks, especially when pushed down their turrets.

France and Britain both organised the sending of weapons and materials to help the beleaguered Finns, and they also set about raising a small expeditionary force to help them out on the ground, but they could only get there if they crossed through Sweden and Norway. Sweden just happened to be a vital source of iron ore for Germany, in the summer months these supplies could be transported via the Baltic which was out of reach of the Allies, however in the winter the Baltic route froze over and the iron ore had to be shipped by rail to Norway and then shipped down the Norwegian coast to Germany. In Hitler's eyes, if the Allies were allowed to cross the continent en route to Finland they could also interfere with their iron ore supply – and that simply wouldn't do. Also, if the Russians managed to capture Finland, that would put Stalin dangerously close to these Nordic supplies. Hitler had no choice but to make the first move.

In the small hours of 9 April 1940 the Danish and Norwegian governments were handed an ultimatum which they were forced to accept immediately. Even as the documents were being read the German Army were going through the final checks before they set off to smash Scandinavia. The Danes didn't have a hope, there was no way they could defend themselves against the might of the panzers (German tanks) and before most Danish citizens had woken up that morning they had effectively surrendered to the Nazi military machine.

In Norway, however, it was a bit different.

Despite all the key ports and coastal towns falling into German hands within hours of the initial advance, the king of Norway and his government refused to capitulate. The Nazis tried to talk the king into doing what they saw as 'the right thing' and handing his country over to Hitler, however their tactics soon switched from flattery to intimidation and when neither of those worked they resorted to trying to wipe him off the planet. The king and his entourage were forced to flee into the forests whilst the Kriegsmarine (the German Navy) started to bombard Oslo.

Meanwhile the British had regrouped and were trying to kick the Germans out of the Norwegian town of Narvik; on 10 April five British naval destroyers faced off against ten German destroyers in the surrounding waters. In the ensuing firefight each side lost two destroyers with the Royal Navy also scoring a number of hits on enemy merchant ships plus an ammunition carrier. Two days later the two navies went at it again at Narvik, this time the Royal Navy emerged as convincing winners – HMS *Warspite* and nine other naval destroyers attacked eight enemy destroyers and sank or damaged every single one of them. This victory enabled significant numbers of British troops to be landed in Norway, however they were badly supplied and poorly organised and didn't make the most of their opportunity. With the threat of a Nazi invasion in Western Europe becoming more and more real, British and French priorities were beginning to shift away from Scandinavia. Eventually they withdrew all support, leaving the Norwegians to continue the fight on their own.

Hitler now had Norway in his pocket – but at a cost. The Kriegsmarine had lost a lot of ships, including the pocket battleship *Lützow*, leaving a rather large hole in its fleet for the rest of the war.

10 May 1940 was an interesting day. In Britain, Winston Churchill replaced Neville Chamberlain as prime minister. Meanwhile on the continent, Germany initiated the invasion of Belgium, the Netherlands and Luxembourg.

Case Yellow: Invasion of the Low Countries, 1940

Although ultimately victorious, France had taken an absolute beating during the First World War and after the Treaty of Versailles the whole nation was determined never to go through such an experience again. The top brass in the French military knew that German anger over the terms of the treaty all but guaranteed some kind of revenge attack in the future and they quickly put their heads together in an effort to come up with ideas that would negate a second wave of German aggression. Under the direction of War Minister André Maginot and with the backing of Marshal Pétain, the French set about constructing a huge line of concrete fortifications along their eastern borders with Switzerland, Luxembourg and Germany.

This defensive line – called the Maginot Line – was not a continuous line of fortifications and defensive outposts. Altogether there were about 500 separate defensive positions, including fifty large forts (known as *ouvrages*) that were positioned along the frontier at every nine or ten miles. Each *ouvrage* could house up to 1,000 soldiers, was designed to withstand numerous direct hits and bristled with artillery that could cover the nearest two *ouvrages* to the north and to the south. There were also thousands of miles of anti-tank ditches, machine-gun posts and mine fields. In total, over half a million French soldiers were employed with the express order to repel any German attack. It was, when all's said and done, an impressive defensive wall, apart from one tiny aspect – it left a Belgian-sized gap to the north where no fortification was built. The Maginot Line was incomplete.

To be truthful, there was never any plan to build all the way through to the channel because the French wanted to protect Belgium's neutrality and, anyway, that part of their border was also protected by the Ardennes Forest – an area generally considered impenetrable. There was absolutely no way the Germans would attack through there. Was there?

At dawn on 10 May 1940, Case Yellow – the German invasion of Holland, Belgium and ultimately France commenced. As the Luftwaffe roared through the skies unmolested, German guns barked into life on the Western Front once more.

Getting ready to march into Belgium, Holland and France were 136 German infantry divisions, backed up by an impressive and dominant Luftwaffe that boasted over 3,500 aircraft. Allied ground forces totalled 135 divisions, ninety-four of which were French. On paper this may have seemed like a fair fight, but in reality the French Army was a shadow of its former self. They had once been at the forefront of motor transport in warfare, yet in 1939 had seemingly gone backwards and relied heavily on railways and horse transport. Conscripts were poorly trained, ill equipped and badly disciplined. When the Germans commenced their advance, the French High Command immediately went on the defensive, ignoring Napoleon's own maxim:

'The side that stays within its own fortifications is beaten.'

The offensive started in spectacular fashion with a lightning air strike over Holland. Airborne troops captured important bridges across the Maas Estuary – effectively cutting the country in two. Dutch soldiers surrendered in their droves. Further south in Belgium, things were equally spectacular with the astonishing capture of the Belgian fort at Eben-Emael. Regarded as impregnable the fort was the largest and most heavily defended of its kind in the world and was manned by 1,200 highly trained soldiers. Nine German gliders landed on the roof and within hours a small team of airborne troops had successfully captured the fort, destroyed all of its big guns and taken over 1,000 men prisoner. Hitler proclaimed these men as heroes of the Reich and bestowed Iron Crosses and Knights Crosses to many of the men that took part.

Despite all of this, and despite gaining intelligence over the last few days that a large panzer force had been spotted in and around the Ardennes, the French and British troops continued their move north into Belgium.

Meanwhile those panzer forces steadily pushed through the forest. By the evening of the 13th they were knocking on the door of French defenders at the town of Sedan, on the east bank of the Meuse River. It had taken them just three days.

The next morning the Luftwaffe came to pay a special visit to the town of Sedan, but still the French military leaders concentrated their efforts on what they thought was going to happen in Belgium. They were convinced this was where the main German attack would come from, but they were mistaken. By midnight on the 13th, not only were hundreds of German infantry already across the Meuse, but German engineers were also getting busy building bridges to enable their panzer regiments to join them. It would only be a matter of hours before the first panzers rumbled across and had the open fields of France at their mercy.

In Belgium, the British and French forces continued their march, wondering when they would finally get a taste of battle. In reality, the battle was practically over. By the time the French generals had realised what was happening, it was too late. In a desperate panic on 14 May the RAF (Royal Air Force) was sent to the scene in an effort to stop the advance and destroy the pontoon bridges that had been built across the Meuse. Despite their best efforts the Luftwaffe was just too strong, nearly half the Allied planes failed to return back to their base. It was a disaster. In the words of the official history of the RAF:

'No higher rate of loss has ever been experienced by the Royal Air Force.'

The skies above France were undeniably German.

To rub salt into the Allied wounds, on the same day, 14 May, Holland surrendered. Three days later the Nazi war machine rolled into Brussels where the mayor immediately surrendered.

Meanwhile, on the ground outside Sedan, the panzers continued to stream across the bridges. Once across the river the Germans practically destroyed the weak French 9th Army and smashed a hole in the Allied line almost fifty miles wide. French mechanised counterattacks were valiant but ultimately ineffective and by nightfall on 15 May the French were in full retreat.

France needed a miracle.

We Shall Never Surrender! Dunkirk, 1940

The rapid advance into France by German troops is often referred to as a prime example of Blitzkrieg, but the invasion of France wasn't initially planned that way. When it came to France, Hitler and his cronies actually believed that slow and steady would win the race – they wanted to keep the Allies out of Belgium as they were worried that from there they could get at the important Ruhr area and start ripping up vital Germany manufacturing and industrial plants.

Heinz Guderian, leader of the 19th Panzer Corps, had a slightly different opinion however.

Guderian had already smashed his way through the Ardennes in record time and leapt across the River Meuse faster than anyone thought possible – he was a man in a hurry and he wasn't about to slow down anytime soon, thank you very much for asking.

As Guderian led his panzers deeper into France he was joined by another panzer leader on his right-hand side... a certain Erwin Rommel and his 7th Panzer Division. The pace both of these men set as they carved through France was frightening – consistently advancing forty or fifty miles a day. By 18 May Rommel was in Cambrai (the scene of a massive tank battle in the First World War) and Guderian was occupying St. Quentin on the Somme. That same day the Germans occupied Antwerp, the principal port of Belgium. The very next day saw Hitler's elite SS *Totenkopf* (Death's Head) Division get their hands dirty for the very first time in the war as back-up for Rommel's attack at Cambrai, where they came up against a very stubborn bunch of French Moroccan defenders. By the time the soldiers of the SS had finished the job and moved on, they had left behind 200 French Moroccan corpses.

By the night of 21 May, Guderian had arrived at the seaside town of Le Crotoy and in doing so he practically cut off the British Expeditionary Force (BEF) from the main bulk of their French friends and, more importantly, their main supply depots in western France. The Allied forces were now split in two and to the north of the River Somme hundreds of thousands of British, French and Belgian troops were trapped with their backs to the sea and nowhere to go.

Guderian had advanced a staggering 240 miles in just eleven days. The German Army was rampant.

On 22 May Guderian spun to the north and started chasing down the trapped and beleaguered Allied forces that had started to congregate around Boulogne, Calais and Dunkirk. Elsewhere, 22 May was also the day on which the clever chaps based at Bletchley cracked the Enigma code used by the Luftwaffe, however this breakthrough made very little difference to the immediate, desperate situation in France. Back in London, as the Germans advanced upon the trapped Allied troops, Churchill was preparing for the worst. He had already been mulling over the scenario of pulling his boys out of France and back to Blighty and had requested that plans for a full evacuation (codenamed Operation *Dynamo*) be drawn up immediately. In the event of enemy parachute landings in London he had even ordered machine-gun posts to be placed around Whitehall and Downing Street to protect key government positions.

Meanwhile back at the frontline the Allies tried a desperate counterattack, but it was hopeless. They pulled back even further behind the Lys canal system and opened all the sluice gates in an effort to flood the canals and slow the advance of the Wehrmacht (the German Army), but it was no good, the Germans kept coming. The situation was very grim indeed as hundreds of thousands of Allied soldiers were pushed back to the beaches of Dunkirk. By 24 May the Germans had captured Boulogne and surrounded Calais. They had five bridgeheads across the canal and were within striking distance of Dunkirk with very little standing in their way.

Then, inexplicably, on orders from Hitler, the panzers stopped their advance.

Why they stopped has been the subject of much beard stroking among historians ever since. No one really knows for sure, although there are a few reasons that may have caused this decision. Firstly, the German army had been on the march for weeks without much of a break. Supply chains needed to be patched and weary legs rested. Secondly, the Germans thought that only 100,000 men were trapped at Dunkirk and that the bulk of the Allied forces were still in the south heading back to Paris, so this was their main focus initially. Thirdly, Guderian was nervous about sending in his panzers across the soft marshy lands around Dunkirk, he preferred to wait for a few reinforcements and save his machinery for the run on Paris. Added to which, Göring had convinced everyone who would listen that his magnificent Luftwaffe would crush any attempt at an evacuation across the Channel. For the Germans there was no real sense of urgency; those men on the beaches were going nowhere – the war was practically done and dusted.

But, whilst the Wehrmacht (the Germany Army) paused for breath, an evacuation of monumental proportions commenced. On 24 May 1,000 men were safely evacuated from Boulogne and on 26 May Churchill gave the nod to allow Operation *Dynamo* to begin. On 27 May the first vessels sailed across the Channel – thirty-five craft were involved and they rescued 7,669 men – a valiant effort, but with the Luftwaffe knocking seven bells out of Dunkirk from the air, the rescue needed to be much grander in scale. More boats were needed. Fast.

In a scene reminiscent of Lord Kitchener's famous 'Your Country Needs You' appeal for more men during the First World War, the call went out for boats. Any boat that could get to Dunkirk and back safely would do – fishing boats, pleasure boats, paddle steamers, speed boats, yachts... anything. The response from the public was nothing short of incredible with vessels of all descriptions from as far afield as the West Country and the Isle of Man happily volunteering to help get the boys back home.

Over the following days almost 700 British ships ranging from Royal Navy cruisers to tiny tug boats sailed to and from Dunkirk picking up the battered remains of the BEF. Despite the best efforts of the RAF to keep the Luftwaffe busy in the skies above (they lost 106 aircraft during the operation), the beaches and loading areas were bombed and strafed incessantly from the air during this time. Very quickly sunken boats were blocking embarkation points and it was getting more and more difficult for the men to physically get on board the waiting vessels. During the evacuation period 226 rescue boats were sunk.

Despite all of that, 338,226 men (including around 120,000 French and Belgians) were successfully rescued from the beaches and port of Dunkirk between 27 May and 4 June.

It was a miracle.

As the last of the ships were unloading their rescued cargo on 4 June, Winston Churchill addressed parliament and delivered what is widely acknowledged as one of the finest oratorical moments in British history:

'Even though large tracts of Europe and many old and famous States have fallen or may fall into the grip of the Gestapo and all the odious apparatus of Nazi rule, we shall not flag or fail. We shall go on to the end. We shall fight in France, we shall fight on the seas and oceans, we shall fight with growing confidence and growing strength in the air, we shall defend our island, whatever the cost may be. We shall fight on the beaches, we shall fight on the landing grounds, we shall fight in the fields and in the streets, we shall fight in the hills; we shall never surrender...'

For Britain, Dunkirk was a disaster turned into a triumph (of sorts) and for the BEF it marked the end of a very painful and costly episode. For the French, however, the agony continued.

Avenging Versailles: The Fall of France, 1940

After Dunkirk the Wehrmacht turned its attention to the capture of the rest of France. In order to get a ringside seat for the upcoming show, Hitler moved his headquarters to the Belgian village of Brûly-de-Pesche and got busy planning the downfall of the French. On paper at least it looked like a formality. The beleaguered Allied Commander-in-Chief General Weygand found himself with just sixty-six divisions at his disposal and facing a massive enemy force of 120 divisions with another twenty-three in reserve just for good measure.

The Battle for France officially got going on 5 June 1940, Hitler and his fellow Nazis were confident that they would be enjoying copious amounts of *vin rouge* in Paris in a matter of days. Initially, however, it wasn't quite as easy as they had expected. Rommel's 7th Panzer Division ran into fierce resistance and suffered considerably. The French were well organised, took up decent defensive positions and were fighting for every inch of ground.

Somehow, the spirit of Verdun had returned to the French Army.

Unfortunately for the French, the sheer numbers of their enemy proved too much. By 8 June Rommel's men had reached the River Seine, to his left the German Ninth Army had crossed the Chemin des Dames and on his right the 15th Panzers had put the French Tenth Army to the sword. The French were under huge amounts of pressure right across their country and were forced to execute a tactical retreat in an effort to find a decent defensive position, giving up huge areas of land in the process.

By 12 June Weygand had only twenty-seven active divisions, he was forced to retreat once again but in reality the writing was on the wall. The Nazis walked into Paris unmolested on 14 June 1940 – the city was practically empty as the vast majority of Parisians had already left. At that point, Churchill ordered the immediate evacuation of all British troops in France and 30,600 men were shipped home from Cherbourg on 15 June.

Twenty-four hours later, with the Germans advancing quickly all over France, the French Premier Paul Reynaud resigned and was replaced by First World War hero Marshal Pétain. One of the first things Pétain did was to ask the Germans (and the Italians who had declared war on Britain and France on 10 June) for an armistice.

Sensing an easy victory when most of the hard work had already been done, Mussolini ordered 450,000 men of the Italian First and Fourth armies to attack the southeast portion of France between the Mediterranean and Mont Blanc. The Italians moved forward on 20 June, facing them were 185,000 French defenders under the leadership of General René Olry. Once again, on paper it looked like the French were going to be on the receiving end of a bit of a beating.

However, the Italians were not in the same class as the Germans and struggled to break through more than a mile or two beyond the French line. Elsewhere, the Italians failed to make any progress at all, despite huge numerical advantages. General Olry succeeded in keeping the Italians out of France and remarkably only lost thirty-seven men killed and forty-two wounded, compared to 631 Italian dead and 2,631 wounded. It was an embarrassing loss for the Italians.

Hitler was not impressed.

The mood of the Nazi leader improved somewhat on 22 June when a French delegation, headed by General Charles Huntziger, signed the armistice that formally signalled the complete surrender of France. Hitler had arranged for the original railway carriage in which the 1918 Armistice had been signed to be brought up from Paris to the same forest in Compiègne and set up just as it had been for the German surrender.

It was a clear and symbolic act of revenge.

Hitler made a point of sitting in the very seat that Allied Supreme Commander Marshal Foch had sat in twenty-two years earlier as the formalities were carried out by Field Marshal Wilhelm Keitel. He didn't say a word; he didn't have to. After the terms of the surrender had been given to the French, the German delegation exited the carriage to the sound of the German national anthem, leaving a tearful group of French leaders to contemplate the future in which two-thirds of France was given over to Germany and the French Army was completely disarmed.

At 18:50hrs on 22 June 1940 Huntziger signed the document. The Battle of France was over. France had lost almost 100,000 men killed, approximately 250,000 wounded and 2 million men taken prisoner. Germany had lost 27,074 dead and 111,034 wounded.

As soon as the ink had dried on the surrender document, Britain readied for invasion.

Pots, Pans and Invasion Plans, 1940

On a clear day the Germans who occupied Calais could see Dover just twenty-two miles across the water. Bearing in mind how quickly they had just smashed through France and the Low Countries, any German officer would have been forgiven in thinking that it was just a matter of time before he would be putting his feet up in the 'Garden of England', enjoying fish and chips and a couple of pints of local ale.

Indeed, across the Channel there was a very mild sense of panic as the whole country made plans for the worst-case scenario: invasion.

Thousands of children living in Kent, London and the south of England were evacuated to safer areas and a million men, deemed too old or unfit for regular army service, were brought together to form a 'Home Guard'. They drilled with broomsticks because there were not enough rifles to go around and they practised tactics that were sure to give Adolf and his mates a less-than-friendly welcome if they were ever to decide to drop in for a cup of tea and a cream bun.

Anti-tank barricades were erected all over the place, and signposts and place names across the country were either defaced or removed in an effort to confuse any would-be invader. The beaches and the countryside areas of the invasion zone practically disappeared under a sea of barbed wire and defence works. It wasn't quite the Atlantic Wall but it was nonetheless a formidable set-up, which was more than could be said for the British Army.

The truth was, after Dunkirk, the British Army was in a bad way; the men may have escaped from the beaches with their rifles, but they were forced to leave an enormous amount of kit and equipment behind. In June 1940 the only fully fitted and equipped division in Britain was Canadian. In the whole of the southeast of England (widely thought of as the most likely area for an enemy invasion at that time) there were no anti-tank weapons of any kind and not one single tank.

The cupboard was bare.

Whilst the rest of the country held its breath, the manufacturing and munitions plants were working 24/7 to re-arm the army and air force. The call went out for all members of the public to contribute to the war effort by donating their pots and pans – the premise being that they could be melted down to make tanks, fighter planes and such things. All over the country people donated their cooking utensils, resulting in mountains of pots and pans. Iron railings and metal fencing were also taken. How much of this stuff was actually melted down and used for manufacturing is still debated today, it is likely that only a small percentage of what was donated was ever re-used, but the whole initiative certainly got the country working together and made everyone feel that they were doing their bit for the war effort. Meanwhile, the guns, shells, tanks, fighter planes, vehicles, bombs and equipment that were so badly needed were rapidly being stockpiled.

But where was the German invasion?

The truth was that at that time there was no plan to invade. Hitler was too busy celebrating his victory in France to worry about Britain and had even taken a few days out to visit some of the old First World War battlefields he had fought on twenty-five years previously. As far as Hitler was concerned Britain was isolated, alone and probably making plans for a peaceful end to the situation, and if she did prove stubborn and uncooperative, then he would initiate a blockade and starve her into submission. There was no need to worry and after his trip to the battlefields he toured Paris and then returned to Berlin where he was given a hero's welcome.

Meanwhile, both the German Army and the Kriegsmarine began to formulate their own plans for the invasion of Britain. The army plan proposed an initial first wave of 90,000 men that would come ashore via landing zones stretching from Margate in Kent to the Isle of Wight. A second wave of men would be 170,000 strong, plus almost 120,000 vehicles/horses/bikes. To achieve this, the army looked to the Luftwaffe to win control of the air. The plan was tentatively pitched to the Führer on 13 July. Remarkably Hitler didn't question anything and didn't suggest any improvements. It was all systems go.

On 16 July 1940 Hitler issued *Führer Directive No. 16: On Preparations for a Landing Operation Against England*:

> *'Since England, in spite of her hopeless military situation, shows no signs of being ready to come to an understanding, I have decided to prepare a landing operation against England and, if necessary, to carry it out.*
>
> *The aim of this operation will be to eliminate the English homeland as a base for the prosecution of the war against Germany and, if necessary, to occupy it completely...'*

The operation was codenamed *Seelöwe* (Sealion).

Fire in the Sky: The Battle for Britain, 1940

Forty-eight hours after Hitler issued his *Directive No. 16* Winston Churchill addressed the British parliament. He delivered another incredible peroration aimed at inspiring an entire nation:

'What General Weygand has called the Battle of France is over ... the Battle of Britain is about to begin... Hitler knows that he will have to break us in this island or lose the war. If we can stand up to him, all Europe may be freed and the life of the world may move forward into broad, sunlit uplands.

But if we fail, then the whole world, including the United States, including all that we have known and cared for, will sink into the abyss of a new dark age made more sinister, and perhaps more protracted, by the lights of perverted science. Let us therefore brace ourselves to our duties, and so bear ourselves, that if the British Empire and its Commonwealth last for a thousand years, men will still say, **This was their finest hour.**

A few weeks later Hitler issued *Directive No. 17*, 'for the conduct of air and sea warfare against England'. The Führer may have been a crazed megalomaniac, but he knew that the Luftwaffe would need to be masters of the English skies if *Seelöwe* was to stand any chance of success. The whole operation (including the land, sea and air components) was to be codenamed *Adlerangriff* (Attack of the Eagle) and would officially start on *Adlertag* (Eagle Day). The exact day would be decided by the weather.

The chaps at Bletchley Park had intercepted lots of messages that mentioned both *Adlerangriff* and *Adlertag*, and as a consequence they knew something heavy was about to kick off, but they had no idea what.

The 'what' would become known as the Battle of Britain.

Large-scale air operations over Britain had actually begun on 10 July 1940. On that day, sixty Junkers Ju-88 fighter bombers smashed targets at

Falmouth, Swansea and Ipswich, while another twenty-five Dornier Do-17 bombers attacked a convoy of ships in the Dover Straits. Over the next few weeks daily air raids on shipping and military targets continued unabated, however Britain held fast. On 1 August a frustrated Hitler moved the proposed date of Operation *Seelöwe* back a month to 15 September.

Then, on 13 August, Göring changed tactics. He was fed up with the RAF's pesky Fighter Command continually getting in his way as he tried to knock out various ground targets across England. It was now time to blow Fighter Command out of the sky for good.

The Battle of Britain just got serious.

Fighting over England was tough for the Luftwaffe. It wasn't really equipped for a full-scale air war despite Göring's bold predictions. Its bombers didn't have the capacity to carry enough bombs and its fighter planes had enough fuel for just thirty minutes flying time over England before they had to head back to base to fill up again. Not ideal. On the other hand, RAF pilots could land at their airbase, refuel and join the fight again in very short order.

Fighter Command had another distinct advantage over the Luftwaffe. A silent 'ace' in their pack that gave them an undeniable edge over their adversaries – it was called the Dowding System.

The brainchild of Air Chief Marshal Hugh Dowding, this system brought together a network of radar stations, the men of the Royal Observer Corps and one of the most intricate phone systems in existence, which allowed for the early detection of enemy airplanes and the communication of the details of their position and potential flight path to the right people. Quickly. The end result was a huge increase in overall RAF effectiveness. Before the war interception rates of 50 per cent were considered excellent form, during the Battle of Britain the average rate of interception by Fighter Command was 80 per cent.

The Dowding System turned Fighter Command into a lean, mean intercepting machine and contributed greatly to the success of the RAF against the Luftwaffe.

Due to poor weather, Göring had to wait until 15 August before he could put his new plan to subdue the RAF into action. *Luftflotten* 2, 3 and 5 were sent on their merry way with express instructions to smash RAF airfields to pieces from the south coast to Tyneside. Much damage was done, but the Luftwaffe lost seventy-six planes in the process. A similar pattern repeated itself over the next few days, the Luftwaffe was indeed hitting its targets and causing much mayhem and destruction, but it was losing planes and aircrew in the process.

The High Brass of the Luftwaffe didn't seem to mind that they were losing men and machines on a daily basis. Their own intelligence suggested to them that the RAF was also taking a beating. Indeed, by mid-August the Germans were convinced that they were facing an enemy that was practically on its knees with only 300 combat-ready fighters to defend the entire British Isles compared to 2,000 Luftwaffe fighters and bombers. News of this ilk put the German High Command in a very good mood indeed. They were convinced they were winning the Battle of Britain. They were much mistaken.

German intelligence was way off the mark. Fighter Command actually had around 1,100 planes at their disposal with over 800 of them ready to go at a moment's notice to give the Luftwaffe a very British (and Polish and French) spanking.

Blissfully unaware of the actual fighting strength of their enemy, hundreds of Luftwaffe pilots strapped themselves in during the morning of 18 August in preparation to let loose the biggest air storm yet to hit Britain. Many believed this would be the day they finished off the British for good. During the day the Luftwaffe flew an unprecedented 970 sorties over Britain. Fighter bases were smashed and strafed, radar stations were blown to pieces and manufacturing plants were pulverised. The 18th

August was not dubbed 'The Hardest Day' for nothing. Fighter Command was being battered. But it kept functioning. Just.

Despite wave after wave of attacks, very few planes on the ground were destroyed. Vital airfields such as Biggin Hill and Kenley continued to be operational and mobile radar sites were utilised to cover any gaps in the system.

Fighter Command didn't just sit there and take the beating without retaliation. Not likely. It flew 927 sorties of its own – far more than the Luftwaffe thought possible – and put up stern resistance. The Battle of Britain was a battle of attrition, it was the Verdun of the air and on this day both sides lost large numbers of planes. But pilots were more precious than planes; downed German pilots were put straight into prison camps and would never fly in anger again. On the other hand, British pilots were patched up, sent back to their bases and were soon once more on the tail of the Luftwaffe. On 18 August the RAF lost eleven aircrew, the Luftwaffe lost 134.

That same day Hitler postponed Operation *Seelöwe* indefinitely. It may not have felt like it at the time, but the RAF was winning the Battle of Britain.

From 19 to 23 August the weather turned and despite the odd raid here and there the majority of RAF pilots managed to grab a much-needed rest. These few days also gave ground crews up and down the country a window of opportunity to try and fix damaged aircraft, runways, buildings and equipment. Meanwhile back in Berlin Göring grew more and more impatient and started plotting his next 'decisive blow'.

The Blitz was coming.

Britain burns: The Blitz, 1940–41

On 23 August the Luftwaffe launched its fourth massive raid on Britain since *Adlertag* (Eagle Day) with oil factories and manufacturing plants in the south of England among the primary targets. During the raid a small flight of bombers got lost and, worried about the very real prospect of becoming dinner for Fighter Command, they dumped their bombs and headed back home. The problem was they just happened to drop their bombs over London, killing nine civilians.

This apparently unprovoked attack on non-military targets angered Churchill immensely and he immediately ordered the RAF to bomb Berlin in retaliation. On 25 August eighty-one bombers set off for Berlin. Only twenty-nine planes reached their target, no civilians were killed and the physical damage done to Berlin was minimal, but it was enough to put Herr Hitler into a rage of monumental proportions. How dare the English bomb Berlin! They must now be punished!

With his Nazi toys well and truly thrown out of his Teutonic pram, Hitler completely forgot about the strategic imperative of destroying Fighter Command in order to clear the way for Operation *Seelöwe*. Instead he ordered London to be subjected to airborne Blitzkrieg. He announced his intentions to the world on 4 September 1940 during a frenetic speech at the Berlin *Sportpalast*:

'... and if the British Air Force drops two, three or four thousand kilos of bombs, then we will drop 150,000, 180,000, 230,000, 300,000, 400,000 kilos, or more, in one night. If they declare that they will attack our cities on a large scale, we will erase theirs!'

The message was loud and clear: if Britain wanted to dish it out, she had better be prepared to take it.

Britain was about to get Blitz'd.

Shortly before 16:00hrs on 7 September, over 300 German bombers, escorted by over 600 fighters roared up the Thames Estuary heading straight for the London dockyards. Thousands of bombs rained down indiscriminately on to the dockyard areas – smashing buildings, destroying homes and causing massive damage. As dusk fell the skies above London were once more empty but the fires they had left behind roared fiercely on the ground all over east London. Then, at approximately 20:00hrs it was time for the Luftwaffe night shift. It rained bombs until 04:30hrs – it seemed as if the entire city was on fire. Thousands of homes and buildings were destroyed, 448 Londoners were dead with another 1,600 injured. Widespread panic gripped the population. The whole country was put on full alert, ready to face the enemy invasion that was surely just around the corner.

The invasion never actually materialised. Instead London endured what seemed like endless nights of intense bombing by the Luftwaffe. Day two of the Blitz over London saw 200 enemy planes repeat the bombing; this time they targeted power stations and railway hubs. Churchill went to visit bombed-out areas in the East End. Another 412 Londoners died with 747 seriously injured. Day three saw 370 deaths and 1,400 injured – that day King George VI also ventured out to see the devastation in the East End for himself. That night, the RAF sent over significant numbers of bombers to give it back to Berlin, the crew had explicit instructions – even if they couldn't spot their designated military targets, they were not to return to Blighty with their bombs. They were to deposit their payload anywhere they could. That night, Berliners got a taste of the Blitz for themselves. Even Hitler's confidante and Minister of Propaganda Joseph Goebbels's garden received a direct hit.

On 12 September Göring added Bristol, Liverpool and Swansea to his targets with the dockyard areas in all of these cities getting rough treatment at the hands of his bombers. Day after day the raids continued, especially on London. Both Hitler and Göring were convinced that the inhabitants of England's capital would soon crack under the pressure. If

London gave up the fight and the panic spread out across the rest of the country, any subsequent invasion would be a breeze.

But Londoners were tough characters and it would take more than a few Nazi bombers to break them.

To hide from the devastation Londoners fled downwards to the relative safety of the underground. At first the local authorities tried to discourage it, however the sheer weight of numbers got their way and every night thousands of people took refuge in tube stations across the capital. Up and down the country people with gardens constructed simple Anderson shelters made of corrugated iron covered in earth to hide in and in almost every town and city brick-and-concrete civil shelters were built to help the rest of the population. A 'blackout' was instituted every night to try and confuse the enemy bombers and was vigorously enforced up and down the country, not a chink of light was allowed to emanate from any house and no street lights were to be illuminated – the country was plunged into darkness.

Despite the blackout, the Luftwaffe found it quite easy to navigate their way to London every night. They just followed the Thames and it took them right into the heart of the city. In London every single night for the rest of September the bombers came. During twenty-four nights the Luftwaffe dropped 5,300 tonnes of high explosives on the capital. Fires raged almost continuously, roads were smashed, telephone systems destroyed, gas and water mains ruptured, and hospitals damaged. And the death toll mounted, by the end of the month 5,730 people had been killed and 10,000 more had been injured.

During October the perception was that the bombing was becoming less intense. On the night of 6 October only one bomb fell on London. Nevertheless every night the bombers still came. Every night the bombs dropped. Every night the fire crews doused the flames. Every night Londoners picked through the rubble trying to save their possessions and their relatives. The night of 15 October was especially brutal. A full moon lit the way for over 400 bombers to drop over a 1,000 bombs. 430 people were killed with another 900-plus injured.

In the end London was bombed for fifty-seven consecutive nights. After the night raid on 2 November the bombers did not reappear, at least not for a couple of nights. In reality there were only three nights during the whole month when London was bomb-free.

In their efforts to soften up the British population before a massed infantry invasion, the Luftwaffe spread its wings even further and targeted major coastal ports, centres of manufacturing and supply, and numerous cities and large towns. Liverpool, Coventry, Swansea, Portsmouth, Glasgow and Hull all 'enjoyed' a significant piece of Luftwaffe action. During the night of 14t November 1940 Coventry received a particularly brutal visit from 515 bombers of *Luftflotte 3*. The raid was intended to damage Coventry's manufacturing and industrial infrastructure but in the end much more was destroyed. During this one single night the Luftwaffe dropped over 500 tonnes of high explosives and over 36,000 incendiary bombs. At the height of the raid over 200 separate fires were burning and because the water supply had been badly damaged by bombing the local fire service struggled to cope.

The cathedral, 4,300 homes and two-thirds of the city's buildings were damaged. Practically the entire city centre was erased. Approximately 568 people were killed with over 1,200 people injured.

The Blitz claimed around 40,000 lives across Britain with another 40,000-plus injured. Approximately 1.4 million people had been made homeless. On the other side of the fence, during the Battle of Britain and the Blitz the Luftwaffe lost around 2,400 aircraft without achieving any of its objectives.

In May 1941 Hitler called off the attacks on Britain. He was planning something big in the East and he needed his air force to spearhead a new offensive:

Operation *Barbarossa*.

Barbaric *Barbarossa*, 1941

The summer of 1940 saw Hitler and his Nazi regime at the height of their powers. They had conquered practically all of continental Europe and their only real live opponent (Britain) had been vanquished from the mainland and was in no fit state to put up any decent kind of fight. Back in Germany, Hitler was a hero – he had delivered on his promises to rip up the Treaty of Versailles and to regain old German territories (along with a few new ones). The speed of his victories had been astonishing, surprising even the most doubtful army general. They had little room for any future objections to their Führer's plans. And he had some big plans, one of which was a strategy he had set out clearly in his biographical account *Mein Kampf* (*My Struggle*), which he had written years before during his time in prison after the failed coup in Munich. His plan centered on an old German ideal: *Lebensraum*.

Lebensraum was an ideology of territorial expansion originally developed under the old Imperial Empire but was taken to heart by the Nazis. Basically they wanted more space for their perfect Aryan specimens to roam about and be beautiful in, and they didn't really care how they got it. They had eyes on the East – Poland, Russia and the Ukraine – and were very keen to enslave / deport / murder the 'ugly' incumbents of these generously proportioned countries and replace these *Untermenschen* (sub-humans) with their own Aryan master race. The thing was in August 1939 Russia and Germany had shocked the world by shaking hands on a peace agreement (known as the Molotov-Ribbentrop Pact) that stopped them destroying each other. On one hand, this meant that Russia conveniently did not interfere in German 'foreign policy' in Poland, Czechoslovakia and the rest of Western Europe. However, on the other hand, it meant that Hitler had to sit and watch as Stalin got his hands on Finland, as well as Estonia, Latvia and Lithuania which all fell to the Red Army in just a few days in June 1940.

Stalin then went on to grab a big chunk out of Romania, putting him and his Red Army within spitting distance of the German oil supplies at Ploesti.

It was a vital oil supply for Hitler because it was his *only* oil supply. Having the Russians so close to Ploesti got Hitler very jumpy indeed so he looked around for some new friends in order to strengthen his own position in the East and stop Stalin from invading all and sundry.

Bulgaria, Hungary, Yugoslavia and Romania (what was left of it after the Russians had moved in) all joined the Axis in quick succession, moves which annoyed Russia greatly. Then, on 27 September 1940 Germany, Italy and Japan signed the Tripartite Pact in Berlin. The Pact promised that if any of the three would find themselves under attack by any nation not already involved in the war, the others would step in and help. It was primarily aimed at the USA and Britain but it still did not stop Russia protesting angrily – the Molotov-Ribbentrop Pact of 1939 was starting to look a bit shaky.

In an effort to 'clarify the situation' Hitler and Ribbentrop met with Russian foreign minister Vyasheslav Molotov on 12/13 November 1940. They tried to get Molotov to join the Tripartite Pact but the Russian was dubious of Italy's ability to do anything constructive and thought that the Germans were underestimating British resolve. During the talks they had to move out of the Soviet Embassy in Berlin and move to a shelter due to a British air raid. As Ribbentrop tried to insist that Britain was beaten Molotov calmly replied: 'If that is so, why are we sitting in this air raid shelter?'

#harshbutfair

After the meeting Hitler gave the nod to his generals to start planning a large-scale invasion of Russia. On 18 December 1940 he issued *Führer Directive No. 21* which gave formal orders to the leadership of the Wehrmacht and the Luftwaffe to prepare for an offensive war against Soviet Russia immediately – they were to be ready to go by 15 May 1941.

Some of the German Army generals were nervous. They tried to protest about a war on two fronts, something that even Hitler himself had warned against in *Mein Kampf* but Hitler was bullish and not a man to be budged; the Wehrmacht would march against Mother Russia as instructed. Operation *Barbarossa* was on.

The men put in charge of organising the operation were confident of a swift victory akin to what they had achieved in France. The troops were not issued with winter clothing and simple things such as anti-freeze were overlooked. Even the majority of the German civilians believed the Nazi propaganda machine, there was no sense that the country was steeling itself for a savage dogfight. Everyone thought it would be a walk in the park.

How wrong could a nation be?

It all started well enough. Three million German soldiers, along with several thousand tanks were sidled up to the Russian borders with Poland and Romania without incident. It was difficult to hide that kind of troop movement and the impending German invasion of Russia was one of the worst kept secrets of 1941. Churchill sent a telegram to Stalin warning him of the oncoming fight. President Roosevelt also sent a message to Stalin. The missives were ignored; Stalin had a deep mistrust of both countries and thought they were just trying to stir up some trouble. Even his own spies had an inkling as to what was about to kick off, but Stalin chose to ignore all warnings.

Stalin wasn't totally ignorant though. He knew that he would need to fight Hitler at some point. He just wasn't quite ready yet. His army was massive – in 1941 it possessed more weapons than all the other armies in the entire world combined – but the failures against Finland convinced him to try and keep Germany at arm's length for a bit longer to prepare his troops. So he continued to send supplies of raw materials to the Nazis and didn't make any fuss about the massive encroachment of German troops into Soviet-held territory.

It was all in vain though; the biggest land battle in the history of land battles was about to explode into life.

The German plan for *Barbarossa* was simple. Organise more men, more guns, more tanks and more planes than had ever been organised before and launch a continental Blitzkrieg so vast, so violent and so rapid that the Red Army wouldn't know what had hit them. More than 3 million German soldiers would plunge deep into Mother Russia, smashing all before them to pieces. No one would be safe from the German onslaught. The whole purpose of this battle was to get more land and living space for the Aryan race and to destroy the Russian population in the process. This would be a savage battle where civilians were just as much in the frontline as the Red Army infantrymen.

Hitler was supremely confident of victory; the only fly in his Teutonic ointment was of Italian descent. Looking to claim some of the glory, Mussolini tried to 'do a Hitler' and invade Greece. Unfortunately for him Britain came to the help of Greece and stopped any Italian naughtiness in the south, but the thought of the British so close to German-held oil fields in the Balkans caused Hitler many a sleepless night, so much so that he decided to delay *Barbarossa* until he sorted out Greece. This delay of five weeks may have been inconsequential at the time, but turned out in the end to be very costly.

At 03:15hrs on 22 June 1941 Hitler gave the nod to 153 infantry divisions across a vast front of almost 2,000 miles to start mobilising. His men had 3,000-odd tanks and almost 2,000 aircraft at their disposal. The Russians were caught completely by surprise. Russian field commanders up and down the new frontline made frantic calls to headquarters asking for orders, but there were no orders. It was chaos. That morning, thousands of blurry-eyed Red Army infantrymen scrambled out of their tents to find themselves already surrounded by Germans, with no option but to surrender. Within twenty-four hours several panzer divisions up and down the line had already pushed over fifty miles into enemy territory, capturing and securing dozens of strategic bridges and crossings as they went. Three entire Russian infantry divisions were annihilated on that first day, with another five divisions severely mauled. In the air the story was much the same. The first hours of the attack saw a monumental airborne assault in true Blitzkrieg fashion, destroying some 2,500 enemy planes on the ground and many more in the skies.

Within twenty-four hours the world's largest air force had been practically wiped out.

Within a week the Wehrmacht had the proud city of Minsk in their pockets, they were over halfway to Moscow and had bagged themselves almost 350,000 prisoners en route, along with over 3,300 captured tanks, almost 1,800 captured guns and nearly 250 enemy planes. Their three-pronged Blitzkrieg attack was going like clockwork; in the north Army Group North was making a beeline for Leningrad (now St. Petersburg). Army Group Centre (the largest of the three army groups with thirty-three infantry divisions and fifteen armoured divisions) was heading straight for Moscow and Army Group South seemed destined for Kiev.

German armoured columns crossed the River Dnieper on 11 July and with Russian casualties already amounting to the thick end of 1 million men, it seemed as though Hitler was on the cusp of the greatest military victory of all time.

But the Russians kept fighting.

Despite eye-watering casualties there were still plenty of Russian soldiers to go round. In their planning the Germans thought they would be facing roughly 200 infantry divisions (about 3.5 million men) – in actual fact the Red Army had 400 divisions, which meant the Germans had another 3 million angry Russians to contend with. As they plunged deeper and deeper into Mother Russia, extending their supply lines and getting more exhausted by the day, the German invaders kept running into pockets of fanatical resistance that slowed them down and sapped vital energy and resources. The initial speed of those first few weeks suddenly bogged down into a daily grind of intense fighting in hostile conditions on minimal supplies. It was beginning to get very tough indeed.

The common belief held by the majority of German commanders at the time was that a decisive blow on Moscow would be a significant kick in the privates for Russia. Take Moscow and the rest of the country would follow in its wake quite quickly. Everyone agreed with this apart from one person.

Adolf Hitler.

The original plans of *Barbarossa* ordered the capturing of Leningrad in the north and the Ukraine in the south. This, argued Hitler, would be more devastating to Stalin than losing Moscow. So, despite Army Group Centre being almost spitting distance from the city, he ordered them to help in the north and south, and forget about the Russian capital.

This was a big call on the part of the Führer; one that many people think cost his side the war.

His generals were not convinced, but they did as they were told. Army Group Centre halted the advance on Moscow and repositioned tanks, men and resources in order to help the other army groups. By late September Army Group South, with the help of significant firepower from Army Group Centre, had executed what many believe to be the most spectacular pincer movement in history, capturing the city of Kiev and bagging 650,000 prisoners in the process. In the north Leningrad was surrounded and being systematically flattened by Luftwaffe bombs and artillery bombardments. It was only a matter of time before the city surrendered.

With Leningrad on its knees and Ukraine in their pocket, the German High Command once more pleaded with Hitler to allow them to have a go at Moscow before winter set in. This time their Führer agreed but only on the condition that Army Group North completed the capture of Leningrad and Army Group South continued its advance towards Stalingrad. This was not what the Nazi top brass wanted to hear – this meant they would be advancing on three separate fronts across 2,000 miles of terrain, straight into the teeth of the Russian winter while they stretched their supplies and resources to the absolute limit and beyond. They tried to reason with Hitler and asked to be allowed to consolidate their forces for one big strong attack on Moscow.

But Hitler said no.

Meanwhile the small garrison of troops that had been left behind on the approaches to Moscow some two months previous shook off their cobwebs and marched towards the Russian capital. It was 2 October 1941 and there was a definite chill in the air that their summer uniforms were struggling to cope with.

Winter was coming.

Moscow 1941: Zhukov hits back.

Time was not on Germany's side. If the Germans wanted to spend Christmas in Moscow sipping vodka, they needed to get a move on and capture the city before the winter set in. In announcing Operation *Typhoon* Hitler planned to throw considerable resources into the fight – three infantry armies (the 2nd, 4th and 9th) supported by three panzer groups added up to more than 1 million fighting men 1,700 tanks and 14,000 guns. Reinforcing from the air would be *Luftflotte 2,* which although it had only around 550 operational planes, was still a decent enough back up. Facing them would be over 1 million Russians, 1,000 tanks and 7,600 guns. The Russian air force had managed to find 1,000 operational planes from somewhere too and, despite taking a beating in the early weeks of *Barbarossa*, when it came to defending Moscow, the Russian air force had more machines than the Luftwaffe.

This promised to be a tear-up of epic proportions.

The plan was to use classic Blitzkrieg tactics with massed panzer groups (aided by concentrated bombing by the Luftwaffe) rushing quickly ahead, trapping the enemy forces, rounding them up into smaller pockets and annihilating them. It was a tactic that had served the Wehrmacht well since 1939 and the Germans seemed in no rush to move away from its tried and trusted formula.

Initial progress was good. To the north of the city two panzer groups broke through a weak defensive line with no trouble, they met up at Vyazma where they succeeded in encircling four entire Russian army groups in a massive pocket to the west of the city. Now, normal procedure in this type of situation was for the encircled masses to meekly give up and surrender, while the rampaging German invasion force gave them a friendly kick in the nuts as they moved on to their next port of call.

But that didn't happen. The encircled Soviet forces fought back. Keeping thousands of German soldiers occupied when they should have been closing in on Moscow. Many would-be prisoners even managed to escape and retreat back to bolster the defensive lines of Moscow.

To the south, at Bryansk, it was a similar story. The Red Army in this part of the front was quickly encircled and Bryansk fell on 6 October. But again the Soviet troops did not surrender – they kept on fighting, kept on making a nuisance of themselves and kept on distracting the Germans from achieving their main objective. That said, the Germans were ultimately successful in these two initial attacks, they were closing in on Moscow fast now and had bagged themselves another 500,000 prisoners along the way.

Back home in Germany, Goebbels and his mates at the Reich Ministry of Public Enlightenment and Propaganda couldn't contain their excitement any longer. On 9 October they called a press conference at which Nazi press chief Otto Dietrich announced to the international press the news of Moscow's impending fall and with it the collapse of all Soviet resistance. In the eyes of the Germans the fight was practically over. They had won. They had achieved the impossible. They had conquered Russia and it had taken them only a few months.

Only, they hadn't won. The Red Army, although badly battered, was still alive and kicking. Moreover, it had started to snow.

The German Army wasn't prepared for a winter campaign. The Germans were stuck deep in Russia in their summer uniforms without any anti-freeze. On the same day those first snow flurries dusted the ground around Moscow, the capital welcomed a new defender – Stalin replaced the current commander Marshal Timoshenko with General Georgy Zhukov, who had worked miracles at Leningrad and was now in charge of keeping Moscow safe and Nazi free. Zhukov recognised the issues that the Germans would have with the coming weather and so he was content to hold tight to what he had and let Mother Nature do his fighting for him.

As the first covering of snow melted and gave way to torrential rain, the landscape quickly turned to a quagmire. There were very few paved roads outside of the main cities of Russia and it didn't take long for many routes to become so muddy that motor vehicles simply could not move. The Wehrmacht was quite literally stuck in the mud. The only way to move forward was either on foot or by commandeering local horses and wagons. Either way any journey the soldiers undertook was painfully slow and very miserable.

The weather got steadily worse, so much so that the German commanders in the field suggested to Hitler that they paused their advance until the weather improved. But he was having none of it. He would not stop his glorious advance for the sake of a bit of snow! *Nein!* He was convinced he could still achieve total victory before the real winter started so he ordered his generals to keep going. As soon as the ground hardened enough to take the weight of the panzers they were to resume the attack in earnest.

This pause gave Zhukov a window of opportunity to organise Moscow's defenses. However the respite didn't last long. On 14 October a panzer group approached once again from the north, getting to within 100 miles of the city. A few days later another panzer group emerged from the west, just sixty miles out and an infantry division took the town of Gorky, a mere forty miles from the capital. The noose was getting tighter. Rumours of invasion were rife and panic engulfed the citizens of Moscow. Two million of them fled, including most government officials. Even Lenin's coffin was moved to a safe place away from the city.

Stalin, however, stayed put and on 7 November presided over a large parade to celebrate the thirty-fourth anniversary of the revolution. The fact that he didn't run and hide served as a huge confidence boost to his generals and the public at large.

By 15 November the ground was frozen enough to enable the panzers to roll again. Two panzer groups descended from the north with one more coming up from the south with the hope of joining hands east of Moscow. They got close. Very close. German officers could see the spires of the Kremlin through their binoculars but with temperatures regularly in minus thirty degrees Celsius the weather took its toll on German men and machinery. Engines froze, guns froze, men froze and without the correct clothing, lubricants or winter equipment the German war machine simply ground to a halt.

On 2 December a German reconnaissance battalion managed to reach the town of Khimki – just five miles away from Moscow – and captured the bridge over the Moscow–Volga Canal as well as the railway station. It was the closest any German force got to Moscow. The Russians were about to fight back.

On 6 December Stalin unleashed his Siberians in a massive counteroffensive. Forty elite Siberian divisions, trained specifically for winter combat, had been hanging about in the East waiting for a rumble with Japan, however it seemed that Japan had other priorities at this time, so Stalin took the opportunity to re deploy them to Moscow.

It was now time for the Siberians to give the frozen Nazis a damn good kicking.

By January 1942 they had pushed the invaders back by up to 200 miles in places. As the Russians regained their old territory they became aware of the atrocities that had taken place. Public hangings. Mass murder. Whole towns and been wiped off the face of the planet. For many members of the Red Army, it was now time for a spot of revenge. In those first few weeks of the Russian counterattack 300,000 German soldiers were killed. The Russians didn't take many prisoners.

The German assault on had Moscow failed. What was left of the Wehrmacht on the Eastern Front had no choice but to dig in and try and survive the winter.

The Axis Expands: The Balkans, 1941

The fall of France in 1940 brought to the surface a dispute that had been bubbling elsewhere in Europe since the end of the First World War. Since the Treaty of Trianon in 1920 had formally ended the First World War between the Allies and Hungary, Hungary and Romania had been at each other's throats; Hungary had to give Transylvania to Romania, angering about 2 million Hungarians who lived in the area and who had no wish to be ruled by Romania. Consequently they refused to accept any change in their nationality and generally caused trouble for their Romanian governors.

With his precious oil fields in Ploesti, Hitler had been keeping an eye on the situation for a while and when tensions started to rise once more in the summer of 1940 he offered to oversee an amicable end to the dispute.

The result was to split Transylvania into two pieces, plus there was another slight border extension in favour of Hungary. The net result was that 3 million Romanians would now be living under Hungarian rule. Not surprisingly, this outcome didn't go down well in Romania where public pressure forced King Carol II to abdicate and the country began the journey towards fascist dictatorship under the guidance of General Antonescu. To help out his new-found friends, in October Hitler sent his 13th Motorised Division to Bucharest.

This 'occupation' was not well received in Italy where Mussolini was indignant at not being invited to Hitler's Hungarian party, so he decided to throw his own – in Greece. Out of nowhere he ordered his generals to prepare for a full invasion of Greece. On 28 October Hitler travelled to Florence to try and talk his mad friend out of doing something that would overextend the Axis front and create unnecessary risk to his overall strategy in Europe, but it was too late, over 80,000 members of the Italian Army were already on the march and crossing into Greece via Albania.

The problem for Mussolini was that he grossly underestimated the Greek reaction to Italian invasion. He thought they would just roll over and offer no resistance, but the fact was the Greeks hated the Italians, hated Mussolini and wanted nothing to do with his regime. As soon as they realised what was happening, the Greek Prime Minister, General Metaxas, ordered the army to mobilise. It was time to give the Italians a Greek grilling.

Winston Churchill immediately pledged British support for Greece and arranged for reinforcements to be sent across from Egypt. Within a week the Italians had been pushed back across the border to where they came from. The Axis had just been dealt their first defeat in the war.

Meanwhile the Nazi occupation of Rumania had brought the Wehrmacht right up to the Bulgarian border. Not surprisingly this caused a considerable amount of nervousness in the capital Sofia, where seemingly had a choice to make, either get in bed with the Nazis or brace themselves for an invasion that could come at any time. On 1 March 1941 Bulgaria signed up to join the Axis.

Almost immediately Germany established garrisons in Bulgaria, which in turn gave Yugoslavia something to think about. All of her close neighbours were now in bed with Hitler and it was very likely that unless she joined the party she would be carved up between the likes of Hungary, Bulgaria and Italy. Prince Paul of Yugoslavia and his cabinet succumbed to this pressure on 25 March 1941 and joined the Axis, although it was not a popular decision within the military and large aspects of the public. A *coup d'état* was launched on 27 March 1941 that succeeded in replacing the regent with King Peter II. Much to the annoyance of Hitler, who immediately declared Yugoslavia a 'hostile state' and promised to wipe it off the map.

On 6 April 1941 the Wehrmacht launched Operation *Marita* with the objective to carve through Yugoslavia and then march on to Greece to clear up the mess that the Italians had left there with their botched attempt at invasion. Field Marshal Wilhelm List had seven armoured divisions and over 1,000 aircraft at his disposal for this operation, made up of men from Germany, Italy and Hungary. To be honest, even though the Yugoslav Army numbered almost three-quarters of a million men, the vast majority of them were very poorly trained and equipped. They could call on just fifty modern tanks and really didn't stand a chance. By 8 April Lieutenant-General Vieil and his 2nd Panzer Division had already smashed all the way through Yugoslavia and had captured Salonika. Belgrade fell on 13 April after a violent bombardment and four days later the Yugoslav government signed an armistice. Field Marshal List had lost just 151 of his men and had taken over 340,000 prisoners.

Now that the issue of Yugoslavia had been put to bed, List could concentrate the bulk of his forces against Greece. Despite considerable British and Commonwealth reinforcements in the area the Germans quickly gained control of the Greek mainland. Over 50,000 British, Australian and New Zealand troops were successfully evacuated amid being attacked from all sides by crack SS troops and German paratroopers. In many ways the evacuation was even more remarkable than Dunkirk however in the rush to get out the BEF left huge quantities of heavy equipment and supplies. BEF losses amounted to 12,712 men killed, wounded or taken prisoner in Greece; when all was said and done, the whole episode had been a disaster.

With mainland Greece in his pocket, Hitler now eyed up Crete, which was served as a major base for Greek and British forces in the region and was particularly important for its numerous airfields as well as its large harbour at Suda Bay providing an ideal base for naval operations. The German plans called for the use of paratroopers to secure the Maleme airfield in western Crete, with transport aircraft bringing up heavy equipment and reinforcements. Because the Allies had broken the Enigma code, they knew what the Nazis were planning and were able to prepare accordingly.

When the paras began to drop in (it was the largest German paratroop operation of the entire war, with over 10,000 men dropped), Allied riflemen were already in position waiting for them, killing several hundred before they had even landed. Unfortunately for the defenders, the sheer numbers of men falling out of the sky eventually overwhelmed them and the Germans began to make progress on the ground. At Maleme airfield the fighting was bitter with the German attackers failing time and again to shift the New Zealand defenders and take control. They were just about to give up and call it a day when a communications breakdown in the New Zealand ranks caused them to suddenly retreat, basically handing the airfield on a plate to the Germans.

The Germans had captured all of their initial objectives and were launching repeated heavy attacks on the British lines. General Freyberg, commanding the BEF, asked the RAF for support but it was largely ineffective in a rapidly deteriorating situation. Eventually the Allied position on the island was becoming untenable and despite initial opposition from London, Freyberg asked the Mediterranean Fleet to evacuate his men, which was done successfully by 2 June.

Crete was in the hands of the Nazis but it was a costly victory. Of the 22,000 men who took part in the assault 7,000 became casualties and although the operation had proved that airborne assaults could work, it had shown Hitler that they were very costly. In the future any attacks involving paratroopers would also have a heavy infantry involvement too.

Operazione E: The Italians in Africa, 1940

While London and other major British towns and cities were getting a pummeling at the hands of the Luftwaffe, the British government desperately looked around for an alternative way of continuing the fight. An invasion of France was simply not an option; this left the British High Command with two choices. Slug it out with the Luftwaffe in an all-out bombing war or have a go in the deserts of North Africa.

With public morale teetering on the brink, the British government wisely veered away from a prolonged bomb-fest and decided to get to the Axis from the south.

The British had based forces in Egypt since 1882 but out of about 100,000 men in the area only about one-third were ready to fight if the order went out, the rest were in reserve getting ready. Any French armed forces in North Africa were taken out of the equation with the signing of the 1940 armistice. Britain would have to fight in the sand alone.

By June 1940 Italy had amassed a significant fighting force in North Africa including almost 250,000 men, over 1,800 artillery pieces, 150 aircraft and over 300 tanks. All in all this amounted to fourteen Italian divisions. Mussolini fancied himself as a twentieth-century Roman Emperor and wanted to emulate his great ancestors by getting himself his own 'Roman Empire' in Africa – the jewel in such a crown would of course be Egypt. And if he got his hands on a few pieces of Royal Navy hardware as he went, then that would be a bonus.

In the end, when Mussolini gave the nod for his men to invade Egypt on 28 June 1940 (under the codename *Operazione E*), they were up against approximately 36,000 British soldiers. This would not be a fair fight. Certainly the Italians didn't do themselves any favours when their anti-aircraft guns shot down and killed their own commander-in-chief, Marshal Balbo, as he was flying over Tobruk on this exact same day. Balbo was subsequently replaced by Marshal Rodolfo Graziani and, as long as he didn't get shot by his own men too, the invasion of Egypt was set for 15 July – the same day Hitler planned to invade Britain.

Graziani wasn't best pleased with what he had inherited and wanted a bit more time to build up supplies before he attacked. He tried to defer the assault until October but, not surprisingly, Mussolini wasn't having any of it. He did agree to move back the date of the attack to 13 September but only because Hitler had moved Operation *Seelöwe* to 15 September – he was determined to take Egypt on the same day that the Germans landed in Britain. Despite many arguments, Graziani was compelled to start the attack on 13 September as instructed, even though it was obvious that a Nazi invasion on the British Isles wasn't going to happen.

Four Italian divisions plus significant numbers of tanks set off across harsh terrain in temperatures of 50 degrees Celsius. Not surprisingly, despite encountering little resistance, early progress was slow – averaging just twelve miles per day. On 16 September the Italians scored a decent victory as they captured the British supply base at Sidi Barrani after a good showing from their air force, the *Regia Aeronautica*, and the Italian armoured support.

After this mini-victory the Italians had covered sixty miles but they were still 250 miles from their ultimate objective of Alexandria. Graziani wanted to pause for a bit at Sidi Barrani in order to turn it into an effective forward supply base. This disappointed two people: Mussolini because he wanted his men to push on quickly and press home the advantage, and General Sir Archibald Wavell, commander-in-chief of Middle East Command, who wanted his enemy to push on quickly, overstretch their supply lines and become sitting ducks in the desert for a swift British counterattack. Graziani was a seasoned campaigner and knew that his men were willing and mostly able, but their equipment was woefully inadequate. He wanted more guns, more tanks, more men and more fuel; however Mussolini had one eye on the Balkans and was reluctant to send any more men or machines to the desert.

However, by mid-October Graziani still hadn't renewed the attack and his leader was starting to lose patience, threatening Graziani with removal of his command. Yet still the desert commander held firm. He was not prepared to risk his men unless he got his extra resources.

While the Italians were busy arguing, the British were busy getting ready for a counterattack, which they duly launched on 9 December. That day, 36,000 British troops took on an Italian force almost five times as large, with the express intent of kicking them out of Sidi Barrani and the various other fortified camps they had built in the surrounding area. Initially the counterattack was planned to be a five-day raid but at the end of the first day several camps were in British hands as were 38,000 prisoners, 237 enemy guns and seventy-three enemy tanks. British losses were 624 dead. The decision was quickly made to increase the scope of the initial raids to chase the retreating Italians back to where they came from. The Italian Tenth Army was completely routed, suffering thousands of casualties as well as losing 133,298 men prisoner, 420 tanks and 845 guns. In contrast the Western Desert Force lost approximately 500 killed, 1,373 wounded and fifty-five missing.

With Italian positions fading fast, Hitler made a few emergency calls to various members of his High Command.

It was time to send in the Afrika Korps.

Banzai Blitzkrieg: Japan, 1937

The global Great Depression of the 1930s hit Japan hard. The population was growing at about 1 million per year, unemployment was sky high and continued floods ruined harvests and reduced many rural (and some not so rural) areas to near-famine. One of the biggest problems Japan faced was her lack of natural resources – she was completely dependent on foreign oil and mineral supplies to function as a nation – a situation that many influential people in Japan wanted to change.

Emperor Hirohito was idolised as a god by the Japanese public, but he was not an iron-fisted dictator. He was easily manipulated by his army generals who thought the best way to get themselves out of their economic mess was to help themselves to other people's oil.

Hirohito's army bigwigs felt that the Asian mainland offered the best opportunity for economic freedom and had long been active in acquiring territory in that part of the world. They already had Korea in their pockets and after spanking the Russians in the Russo-Japanese War of 1905 they were able to station a significant number of troops in Manchuria. Japan had a soft spot for Manchuria, although it was mostly wilderness it did contain substantial levels of iron ore and coal. Back home in Japan there was considerable pressure on politicians to take what many Japanese thought was rightly theirs as 'spoils of war' but nothing happened. On 18 September 1931 a small portion of the Japanese Army took matters into their own hands.

That day, Lieutenant Suemori Kawamoto detonated a small quantity of explosives alongside a length of railway track owned by Japan near Mukden. The explosion was so weak it didn't even damage the line but the Imperial Japanese Army accused the Chinese of attempted sabotage and duly responded with a full-scale invasion of Manchuria. Resistance was minimal and it wasn't long before Japanese forces controlled the whole country, renaming it Manchukuo. The international community collectively tutted and rolled its eyes, a report sanctioned by the League of Nations pointed the finger at Japan and told her to give Manchuria back to China, much to the annoyance of Japan, who not only told China where to go, but also walked out on the League of Nations.

Back in Tokyo, the shiny brass of the Imperial Army was in feisty mood. Manchuria had been easy to conquer and the international community had done nothing to stop them so they carefully chose the next country on the menu: China.

On 7 July 1937, under the dubious pretext of the kidnapping of a Japanese soldier, the Imperial Army launched an invasion of China. The poorly trained and disorganised Chinese Army was no match for the invaders and within weeks major cities such as Shanghai and Peking were surrendering. It was Blitzkrieg, Banzai style.

Once Shanghai had been taken care of the Japanese troops followed the Yangtze River towards the then capital of China:

Nanking.

Murder, Inc: Nanking

By 9 December 1937 a large Japanese force was knocking on the door to Nanking, the capital of China. Around noon that day the Japanese dropped leaflets into the city that strongly suggested it should surrender within twenty-four hours, and if it didn't things would get messy.

And boy, did things get messy.

After the deadline for the surrender of Nanking passed the Japanese generals signalled the green light for a full frontal attack on the city. By 12 December the Chinese Army was in full retreat under intense artillery and airborne bombardment, twenty-four hours later the Imperial Japanese Army was inside the city walls in hot pursuit. Tens of thousands of Chinese soldiers surrendered and many thousands more tried desperately to blend into civilian life by stealing clothes from the locals. Neither of these acts went down well with the invading forces. The Japanese had long been brought up to believe that surrendering was the ultimate act of cowardice. In their eyes anyone who surrendered had violated an unwritten military code of conduct and in turn they didn't deserve to live.

In the eyes of the Japanese at the time, it was their moral duty to eliminate their newly found prisoners of war (PoW) and they didn't really care if their deaths were quick and easy or slow, brutal and agonising. Many young soldiers were encouraged by their commanding officers to dish out beatings and to inflict as much pain and suffering onto their enemies as possible, for them it was a way of toughening their men up for the forthcoming battles and to rid them of any mercy towards their enemies. Decapitation was common, as were bayonet practices on live prisoners and burning people alive.

You really didn't want to be a Chinese PoW in Nanking in December 1937, but even worse was still to come. After the prisoners had been taken care of, the Japanese turned their attention to the civilian population – specifically the women. For the next six weeks the invaders went on an animalistic rampage of rape, murder, theft, arson, destruction and more rape. All of the city women were brutalised. Young, old, pregnant, it didn't matter to the Japanese. It is impossible to say with certainty but it is estimated over 20,000 women were raped in this six-week period. Most of these were stabbed to death afterwards, forever silencing them.

In a sick contest that was widely reported in the Japanese press both in the run up to the Nanking attacks and during the massacres, two officers, Toshiaki Mukai and Tsuyoshi Noda, set up a little competition between them to see who could be first to kill 100 people with a sword. The local Japanese newspapers kept a running tally of each officer's kills and published their progress regularly during November and December. Both officers supposedly surpassed their goal during the heat of battle, making it impossible to determine which officer had actually won the contest. Therefore they decided to begin another contest, with the aim being 150 kills.

From mid-December 1937 until the end of January 1938 any civilian in Nanking ran the risk of being shot for no apparent reason. There were dead bodies on every street corner. The murder and brutality in Nanking was so bad that even the Nazis told the Japanese to calm down a bit and offered to help mediate between them and the Chinese, but to no avail. Despite the heroic work of a handful of Westerners inside the city who set up a two-mile 'safe zone' and intervened on many occasions to stop the murder of locals, many experts believe that 300,000 people were killed during the Nanking Massacre, however this is a statistic that is incredibly difficult to determine precisely due to the huge number of bodies deliberately burnt, buried in mass graves or simply chucked in the Yangtze River.

This was genocide. Even though numerous eyewitness reports were published in *The New York Times* and *Time* magazine it went largely unnoticed in the West, particularly in Europe where they were too focussed on the potential threat of Nazi rearmament and expansion.

By the end of January 1938 the Japanese were feeling very chipper. They had taken a decent chunk of eastern China and also occupied a number of major cities. However, all of this activity had aroused the suspicion of an old enemy: Russia.

Russia and Japan didn't get on. They had been arguing over borders and territory for years and on 15 July 1938 the Japanese were feeling rather brave and told Russia to remove her border troops from two hills that were on part of the Soviet–Korea border. Not surprisingly Russia ignored the request. Two weeks later Japan tried to take the hills with force and initially looked like they had succeeded in kicking the Russians out of the area. However the Red Army regrouped, gathered in a few reinforcements and gave the Japanese such a beating that they were soon waving the white flag and asking for a peace settlement. For a country that didn't 'do' surrender, this was a humiliating moment.

A year later the Japanese had another go at Russia, this time on the borders with Manchukuo. However, they were going up against a certain Commander Zhukov who came in from the north accompanied by significant motorised and armoured forces. The result was decisive and by the end of August the Japanese Sixth Army had been practically destroyed. Japan would never antagonise Russia again.

The defeat was important as it shaped the future of the war for Japan. She was forced to concede defeat in her quest to get to vital natural resources in the north and she had no choice but to turn her attention to the oil fields and mineral rich resources of Southeast Asia, specifically the Dutch East Indies.

The Great Arsenal of Democracy: America, 1939–41

'... I hope the United States will keep out of this war. I believe that it will, and I give you assurance and reassurance that every effort of your government will be directed towards that end. As long as it remains within my power to prevent, there will be no black-out of peace in the United States.'

President Roosevelt
3 September 1939

When war broke out in 1939 the vast majority of the American population wanted nothing to do with it. To them it was a European war and the Europeans should sort it out. The memories of the First World War were still fresh in their minds. That war had brought too much pain, suffering, disfigurement and death to the population. Nevertheless, the US found herself following a very similar path to the one she trod in 1916, i.e. trying to help Britain and the Allies while trying to remain officially 'neutral'. It was a tough trick to pull off.

Despite intense objections from some areas of the Senate, the US began to sell arms to France and Britain. By doing so Roosevelt was in danger of antagonising Hitler – would the Führer really accept American neutrality when she was selling guns to his enemy? It was a big risk.

After the fall of France, the US drew up the Act of Havana which prevented Nazi Germany getting their hands on any French and Dutch colonies in and around Latin America. Roosevelt was obviously nervous about the state of Europe, and in September 1940 this nervousness turned into mild panic when it seemed that the Luftwaffe would win the Battle of Britain. On 8 September Roosevelt reactivated the draft and called up 800,000 men. The United States of America was placed on full war alert.

The presidential elections of November 1940 were spicy to say the least. Roosevelt was campaigning for a third term in office and was running against Wendell Willkie who was vehemently opposed to American involvement in the European war. Roosevelt's message was the same as it had been since 1939 – one of support for Britain by whatever means necessary, short of going to war. Roosevelt was eventually re-elected and found himself leading a country that was beginning to show signs of sympathy towards the Allied cause.

On 29 December 1940, while the Luftwaffe was once more smashing London to pieces, Roosevelt addressed the people of the United States:

'The people of Europe who are defending themselves do not ask us to do their fighting. They ask us for the implements of war, the planes, the tanks, the guns, the freighters, which will enable them to fight for their liberty and our security. We must be the great arsenal of democracy...'

This was all very well, but the industrialists didn't fancy stopping manufacturing of their own products so they could make guns for a war they didn't care about. They were worried it would lose them market share in their own industry – cars, trucks, machinery, etc. The unions didn't help much either; they dragged their feet on any decision-making in an effort to hamper the war production. Then there were the strikes. Four times as many workers went on strike in 1941 as in the year before. That spring almost half a million coal miners went on strike for a month, and similar action by aviation workers on the West Coast delayed deliveries of planes to Britain by several vital weeks. In some places the army had to be called in to get production going again.

Undeterred, Roosevelt kept on with his plan of helping the Allies. In March 1941 he introduced the Lend-Lease policy under which the US supplied the Allies with food, oil and weapons (including warships and planes). RAF pilots were sent to the US to train and American warships acted as escorts to convoys in the Atlantic. In return, the US was given leases on bases in Allied territory during the war. This programme effectively ended American neutrality.

In the summer of 1941 even though America was reluctant to put the gloves on, it seemed that war was becoming more and more inevitable.

America and Japan were less than friendly. Ever since Japan had first invaded Manchuria, then attacked China and then got in bed with Hitler the Japanese had been struck off Roosevelt's Christmas card list. Shortly after the fall of France, Japanese troops found themselves occupying part of French Indochina, dangerously close to the Philippines which had strong links to America. A nervous Roosevelt immediately ordered an embargo on supplies of aviation fuel and iron ore making its way to Japan but all this did was push Japan even closer to the Axis. On 27 September 1940 Japan joined hands with Germany and Italy by signing the Tripartite Pact with all three members pledging to help each other out if things got difficult with the USA. It seemed like they were ganging up.

Meanwhile back at home in Japan there were rations for civilians, almost every school had some kind of military exercise every day and anything that was deemed to be 'Western' was banned including many sports and most music.

In the summer of 1941 Japan decided to occupy the rest of French Indochina and Roosevelt decided to add oil to the list of embargoed supplies. This left the Imperial Japanese Navy critically short of fuel. Japan now had two choices; either stand down and return home like a bully with a bloody nose or move south and take the rich oil supplies of the Dutch East Indies.

They started to draw up invasion plans almost immediately.

At the same time, the Atlantic US Navy and civilian vessels started to attract unwanted attention from German U-boats. On 11 June 1941 the American freighter *Robin Moore* was sunk by a U-boat. On 4 September the American USS *Greer* became the first US warship to be attacked when *U-652* fired off a couple of torpedoes after it mistakenly thought that the American destroyer had lobbed over a couple of depth charges – they were in fact dropped by a British bomber, but nonetheless, the actions of *U-652* incensed Roosevelt and he ended up telling his navy to shoot on sight. On 16 October the USS *Kearny* was torpedoed by *U-568* while escorting a British convoy. Eleven of her crew were killed. On 31 October the USS *Reuben James* was torpedoed and sunk by *U-552* while she was protecting an ammunition ship en route to Britain with the loss of 115 men. Churchill urged Roosevelt to blow the bugle and declare war, but nothing happened. It would take more than a few sneaky U-boats to draw Roosevelt into a European war.

Then, on 7 December 1941, Japan attacked Pearl Harbor.

Climbing Mount Niitaka: Pearl Harbor, 1941

For Japan capturing the oil fields of the Dutch East Indies intact was going to be hard. Very hard. It would require a massive surprise attack, not just on the oil fields themselves, but also on neighbouring Malaya and the Philippines to negate any counterattacks. After all that they still had to get the oil back to Japan, easier said than done due to a significant Royal Navy presence in Singapore and the massive American naval base at Pearl Harbor in Hawaii.

The Japanese plan to secure the oil was simple. First, destroy the American naval fleet, then, while the US was busy wondering what the hell had happened, quickly overrun the whole of Southeast Asia in a Japanese version of Blitzkrieg. If successful it would mean the Japanese Empire would extend right out across the Pacific and Indian oceans. They would then throw a huge protective air and sea shield around their newly won prizes and start to enjoy the minerals and resources this vast area of earth offered up.

#easypeasyjapanesey

This slightly over-ambitious plan was rubber-stamped by the Japanese government on 6 October 1941.

Sorting out the details for destroying the entire American naval fleet was given to the gifted Japanese Admiral Isoroku Yamamoto. He had at his disposal six aircraft carriers, fourteen other warships, numerous submarines and over 400 assorted attack planes including torpedo bombers. He unveiled his plans to his officers in November on board the battleship *Nagato* and on 26 November the Japanese attack force, under Admiral Nagumo, set sail. On 2 December Admiral Nagumo received a coded message: *Climb Mount Niitaka.* The admiral immediately opened up a set of top-secret documents which contained the irreversible order to go ahead with the attack.

Pearl Harbor was about to get a pasting.

Eleven days after setting sail, the attack fleet had covered 4,000 miles completely undetected and was gathered just 200 miles away from their target. Although US intelligence had cracked Japanese codes and knew that something major was brewing, they didn't know when or where. As a consequence the authorities in and around Pearl Harbor did virtually nothing to improve security of the fleet anchored there, nor did they do much to protect the numerous aircraft that were parked out in the open all around the base. They were convinced that, whatever the Japanese were up to, there was no way they would have the guts to attack Hawaii.

They were badly mistaken. At 06:00hrs the first of over 400 torpedo planes and bombers took to the air. The war was about to go global.

At 07:15hrs the formation of aircraft was spotted on American radar but an officer at the local information centre told the radar team not to worry about it, saying it was a group of B-17 Flying Fortresses – it was a missed opportunity to raise the alarm. At 07:55hrs on the morning of Sunday, 7 December, the first wave of enemy aircraft came rushing in from the Pacific. When the air raid sirens rang out across the base the American defenders were caught in a slight daze. They weren't expecting an attack; they weren't prepared for an attack. What the hell was going on?

Most of the warships in the docks had only a scratch crew on board, the airplanes in the base were not ready for a fight, even the anti-aircraft guns were not fully manned, their ammunition boxes were locked and the crews did not have the keys.

The next two hours were complete mayhem.

Initially the Japanese attacked the airplanes on the ground in an effort to limit any air defense. Moments later torpedo bombers attacked the American fleet anchored just off shore. Every single American battleship that was in the harbour that morning was either sunk or damaged and eleven other warships were either sunk or put out of action. Within twelve minutes of the attack starting the USS *Oklahoma* had suffered five direct torpedo hits and had listed so badly she was practically upside down, over 400 of her crew were killed or missing. Shortly afterwards USS *Arizona* suffered an explosion in her forward ammunition compartment and sank with the loss of 1,177 crew.

After an hour, the first wave of attackers disappeared back to their carriers, however there was no respite for the defenders of Pearl Harbor as wave two was already knocking on their door. Over 130 bombers and thirty-six fighters continued to batter the US fleet as well as air bases and flying boat bases around the perimeter. Then, after 110 minutes of utter carnage, the skies above Pearl Harbor went quiet. The Americans expected a third wave of attacks, many Japanese officers urged Nagumo to make the most of the opportunity and launch another attack to destroy as much of Pearl Harbor's fuel depot, maintenance stores and dry dock facilities as possible. Despite the clamour for another go, Nagumo decided to call it a day. He believed that the mission had been a success and running another sortie risked losing men and machines. The American anti-aircraft guns had been quite productive during the second attack, plus any pilots returning back successfully from a third stint would probably have to land on their carriers in the dark – for him, this was too much of a risk.

It was time to head back to Japan.

Total American casualties that day were 2,403 killed and 1,178 wounded. Two battleships had been completely destroyed, along with one other vessel, and sixteen others had been badly damaged. The Japanese had either destroyed or damaged 318 US aircraft. Even though the US Navy's three aircraft carriers had not been in port and had escaped the attack, it had been a bad morning for America.

In contrast, Japan had lost just twenty-nine aircraft and five midget submarines. Sixty-four men were dead and one, Ensign Kazu Sakamaki, whose midget submarine ran aground, was taken prisoner – he was the first Japanese prisoner of the Second World War. All in all this was a relatively small price to pay for such an astonishing offensive.

Despite American and British declarations of war, the Japanese war machine marched on through Southeast Asia, getting closer and closer to the oil fields and total domination of the region.

For Hirohito and his generals, it was all working out beautifully.

Dancing with the Devil: Wannsee, 1941–44

As well as fighting with the Russians in the East and the Allies in the desert, the Nazis were also waging another kind of war. A war hell bent on exterminating international Jewry.

To anyone who had been listening to what Hitler and his cronies had been screaming about since the early 1930s it was no surprise that Jews were on the receiving end of some incredibly brutal treatment at the hands of the SS and the Gestapo. However, by the time the Wehrmacht had started its journey into Russia the Nazis view on Jews, Slavs and other so-called *Untermenschen* (sub-humans) had reached a whole new level.

The reasons behind such intense hatred of an entire race of people were as complex as they were delusional. Many war veterans (of which Hitler was one), firmly believed that the Jews had betrayed Germany in 1918. Very quickly, even though in the early 1930s Jews accounted for less than 1 per cent of the German population, they were blamed for everything. They were blamed for left-wing politics, they were blamed for pedalling exploitative capitalism, for degenerate cultural ideals and for the secularisation of the population. You name it, it was their fault. Adolf Hitler and the young NSDAP party were very quick to fan the fire, ensuring that the general public perception of Jews was in keeping with their own warped view.

Fast-forward a decade and Hitler's views had becoming even more sickening and warped. In his eyes the Jews were responsible for the expansion of the Second World War. He was convinced that Jews were intrinsically involved in both Bolshevism and capitalism and that the top men of both the US (Roosevelt) and the USSR (Stalin) were just pawns in a game that 'international Jewry' was playing out in a bid for world domination.

In the early days of the war the Nazis rounded up as many Jews as possible and put them in special camps somewhere remote so they could not 'infect' the rest of the Third Reich, it was this way of thinking that gave birth to the building of ghettos. One of the largest ghettos was built in Warsaw where 380,000 people were crammed into a tiny area of the Polish capital. Completely sealed off from the outside world, the people imprisoned within its walls were exposed to acute hardship, hunger and disease. Thousands died.

In June 1941, shortly after the start of Operation *Barbarossa*, a memo was sent to all senior officers telling them all in no uncertain terms that: *'This battle demands ruthless and energetic measures against Bolshevik agitators, guerrillas, saboteurs, Jews and a complete elimination of any active or passive resistance.'* And this was the message sent out to the regular army; the instructions given to the SS were far more disturbing.

Hot on the heels of the Wehrmacht invasion force in Russia were special *Einsatzgruppen* (extermination groups) made up primarily of SS and German police that had a very special job: the murder of Jews, Communists and other perceived enemies of the state. The way they went about their work was crude but effective, basically rounding up their victims, moving them to a pre-designated killing area and then shooting the lot of them.

By the autumn of 1941 the Nazis were travelling along a path that had never been explored before. They had consciously decided to exterminate an entire race. If we are able, with our knowledge of the horror they wreaked, to leaving all emotion at the door, what they were trying to do had the potential to be a logistical nightmare. If they were to succeed in this task they needed to have an efficient process in place and many questions were still unanswered.

In an effort to sort all of this out, Reinhard Heydrich, Chief of the Reich Main Security Office, invited fourteen handpicked Nazi officials to join him in a large villa on the shores of Lake Wannsee in an effort to thrash out a 'final solution' to the Jewish question. The meeting took place on 20 January 1942 and has become known as the Wannsee Conference.

SS-Obergruppenführer Heydrich had been given the nod by Göring to build the process that would enable the Nazis to destroy the Jews in Europe. During the Wannsee Conference he advised his fellow Nazis that he had calculated that there were 11 million Jews in Europe, half of which were living outside of the Reich. He spoke for an hour and then the group discussed the whole situation for another thirty minutes.

A copy of the minutes of the meeting – taken by Adolf Eichmann – survives, so we know exactly what they discussed. For example, Otto Hofmann (Head of the SS Race and Settlement Main Office) and Wilhelm Stuckart (State Secretary of the Reich Interior Ministry) both pointed out the legal and administrative difficulties of mixed-race marriages and suggested compulsory dissolution of mixed marriages or the wider use of sterilisation as an alternative to stop these people having children. Erich Neumann (a director from the office of the Four Year Plan) argued for the exemption of Jews who were working in industries vital to the war effort, Heydrich assured him such Jews would not be killed. Josef Bühler (State Secretary of the General Government) offered his support for the plan and hoped the killings would commence as soon as possible.

Towards the end of the meeting, the men were served cognac and soon the conversation became less restrained – they all talked openly about the subject, discussing ideas on different methods of killing.

The meeting was not designed to agree or disagree about whether to kill Jews or not, that decision had been taken a long time ago, the real reason was to talk through the practicalities of the process and to make it clear that from now on the Final Solution to the Jewish question was a matter for the SS and the SS alone. No one present voiced any concerns. Heydrich was effectively given carte blanche.

As a result of the conference extermination camps were built at Treblinka, Sobibór, Chelmno, Majdanek and Belzec during 1942. Auschwitz, already set up as a work camp, was given a huge new extension (Birkenau), which also held extermination and cremation facilities. It is almost impossible to get completely accurate numbers but it is estimated that these camps murdered anywhere between 2,700,000 and 3,000,000 Jews before the end of the war, with 1,000,000 dying at Auschwitz alone. At Auschwitz, the primary killing method was gas in the form of crystals that were poured into large rooms through special openings in the roof. Once in contact with the air the crystals vaporised and turned into a highly toxic gas that made short work of anyone breathing it in. The Nazis viewed it as an efficient and clean method of extermination.

The genocide of European Jews was organised from Berlin but the programme could not have been carried out so successfully without the help of many non-German accomplices. In Romania where there was also a long-standing culture of anti-Semitism, the war against Russia provided the perfect backdrop to deport and/or murder large numbers of Romanian Jews. In the Ukraine and other Baltic states the invading German Wehrmacht found teams of enthusiastic local police or militia more than willing to hunt down and murder Jews on their behalf. In France, the French Vichy government, along with the French police, managed to round up and deport 75,000 Jews – the vast majority of these were killed in death camps.

Denmark was practically unique in managing to secretly ship almost all Danish Jews over to Sweden without being found out. Hungary resisted gamely all demands for deportation until 1944 when German forces finally occupied the country. It is estimated that half of the Jewish population of Hungary died in the gas chambers of Auschwitz.

All in all it is estimated that around 5,000,000 human beings were killed during the Holocaust.

Kings of Asia: Japan Rampant, 1942

Emperor Hirohito and his military commanders would have thoroughly enjoyed Christmas 1941. The US Navy fleet had been badly mauled at Pearl Harbor, which meant they were now kings of the Pacific. They didn't hang about pressing home the advantage either on the very same day as their torpedo bombers were doing their best to put the US fleet at the bottom of the sea, Japanese bombs were being dropped on Singapore and Japanese infantry were wading ashore at Kota Bharu in Malaya and in Thailand. Twenty-four hours later the Japanese 38th Infantry Division knocked on the door of the British garrison in Hong Kong.

On hearing the news that the Japanese were on the prowl near Hong Kong the Royal Navy dispatched two battleships – HMS *Repulse* and HMS *Prince of Wales* – along with a number of destroyer escorts in an effort to give the invaders a nice surprise as they were trying to get their men and supplies ashore. However this small armada was spotted by an enemy submarine who sent details back to Rear Admiral Matsunaga who immediately organised a surprise of his own for the Royal Navy, consisting of over fifty torpedo planes and over thirty bombers. With no RAF cover, the Royal Navy ships were in all sorts of trouble – both *Repulse* and *Prince of Wales* were sunk and 840 men were lost.

The Japanese were completely dominant. On 8 February 1942 they had the audacity to invade Singapore – a lucrative British stronghold for more than a century with a decent British garrison of 130,000 men, five times that of the invading Japanese force. It took just one week for the Japanese to own Singapore. They may have had less men, but they had tanks. Two hundred to be exactly, whereas the British had precisely zero. The Japanese also enjoyed air superiority which greatly aided their victory. Some 80,000 British, Indian and Australian troops were taken prisoner at Singapore. Their fighting might have been over, but they were about to walk into a world of forced labour, starvation and appalling cruelty at the hands of their captors.

It wasn't just the British Empire that was taking a beating. The US garrison islands of Guam and Wake were also forced to surrender. Borneo fell too and General Wavell, now Commander of the Allied forces in Southeast China, was forced to move his headquarters to Ceylon (now Sri Lanka). Next on the list for the Japanese was the island of Java. The Allies saw an opportunity to intercept the invasion convoy and a small fleet containing fourteen vessels including the British heavy cruiser HMS *Exeter* and the American USS *Houston* was sent to off to make a nuisance of themselves.

Unfortunately the Allied fleet had no air cover, in total ten Allied ships were lost, along with over 2,000 sailors. The Battle of the Java Sea was a complete and utter disaster, signalling the end of any effective Allied naval presence in Southeast Asia. The Japanese invaded Java on 28 February, on 9 March the Dutch and Allied forces on the island surrendered. With Java in their pockets the Japanese had possession of the entire Dutch East Indies and were now by rights the fourth largest oil producer in the world.

Japan was rampant, and it was now time to kick the US out of the Philippines for good and move on towards Burma.

In the Philippines the Japanese had been asking the Americans to surrender since the middle of January, but General Douglas MacArthur, Field Marshal of the Philippine Army, was having none of it. Instead, in the face of overwhelming numbers, he dug in even deeper and gritted it out. By the end of February the Americans were still hanging on, just. They were desperately short of ammunition, medical supplies and food and Roosevelt had to demand that MacArthur get out of there to the safety of Australia. He needed his best generals to fight another day, not get taken prisoner. Reluctantly, MacArthur handed over command to General Jonathan Wainwright and left with this family and staff. After a hazardous journey they made it safely to Mindanao where he vowed to return to the Philippines as a liberator.

Meanwhile, back on the ground, the US troops were in all sorts of trouble. The Japanese demanded surrender once more on 1 April, but again the Americans ignored it. The Japanese attacked once again, this time – with the Americans weakened by general exhaustion, a lack of food and dysentery – they managed to break through. On 10 April the US surrendered and 12,000 men were taken into captivity. It was the largest surrender in US military history.

Burma was another territory that Japan eyed up due to oil, but that was not the only reason. They also wanted to control the 'Burma Road' – an important supply route for the Chinese Nationalist Army via which they received vital equipment, mainly from the US. Burma was garrisoned by a weak British and Indian force and although they tried desperately to cling on, they were badly outnumbered, poorly equipped and had no air cover. The British were forced to retreat through jungle, terrain which the Japanese were very comfortable in, unlike the Brits, who hated every step of the thousand-mile trudge. By early March 1942 Rangoon had been abandoned and on 29 April two Chinese armies that had been moved in as reinforcements had been routed. There was no other choice but to retreat back to India. Burma was lost.

By mid-1942 the Japanese were in control of almost everything they had set out to conquer in their plans of November 1941. They were without doubt the undisputed champions of Southeast Asia.

U-boats: The Battle of the Atlantic, 1941–42

After the fall of France, Churchill was a worried man. Not only because of the direct threat of a full-scale Nazi invasion, but also because of the prospect of German U-boats patrolling the Atlantic sea routes that were vital for supplies of both food and war materials from North America. If the Nazi U-boats could prevent ships carrying supplies to Britain there was the very real possibility of civilian starvation and absolutely no chance of the Allies getting enough kit together to launch any major offensives in mainland Europe.

Churchill was so worried that in March 1941 he set up a committee that met daily to try and snuff out the U-boat and Luftwaffe threat to this vital naval supply route. With forward bases on the French and Norwegian coasts, and with new long-range planes spotting likely targets for the U-boats, the Germans posed a huge threat. On top of this, Admiral Karl Dönitz had perfected his 'Wolf Pack' strategy, in which groups of U-boats attacked at night on the surface where they could not be detected by Allied sonar. Convoys were especially vulnerable within the 'Atlantic Gap', a large area of the mid-Atlantic that could not be reached by anti-submarine aircraft. In this part of the ocean the convoys were on their own. In the last six months of 1940 around 3 million tonnes of Allied shipping was lost. It was a fruitful time for the Kriegsmarine.

The following year wasn't much better for the Allies. British naval records show that around 4.3 million tonnes of shipping (and 1,299 ships) were sunk in the Atlantic during 1941. To counter this loss, Allied shipbuilders managed to put 1.5 million tonnes of shipping back on the water, but the overall amount of available shipping was down by around 2.8 million tonnes. Which was a lot.

That said, there were a few things that happened in 1941 that would have given the Allies cause for slight optimism. The capture of *U-110* (complete with a fully working naval Enigma system and codes) in March 1941 enabled the Allies to track U-boat movements. Neutral America started to behave very un-neutrally in favour of the Allies, with US warships escorting Allied convoys out as far as Iceland and supplying fifty destroyers in exchange for American access to British naval bases. From 11 September US ships were also authorised by President Roosevelt to shoot on sight. On the other side of the fence Hitler ordered the transfer of a number of U-boats to the Arctic Ocean as part of Operation *Barbarossa,* leaving Dönitz very short of wolf packs in the Atlantic, especially in the early part of the year. It wasn't all bad news for the Germans though, because Nazi U-boat production was kicking on nicely and in 1941 there had been 198 shiny new U-boats delivered for active service, which meant that despite the transfers and the losses (thirty-five in total, twenty-seven of which were in the Atlantic) he ended 1941 with more U-boats than he had started with.

#bonus

In 1942 the good times returned to the U-boat teams, with more new vessels being delivered every month and a very naïve US Navy now a legitimate target, the tonnage count ticked over very nicely thank you very much. In the first six months of the year over 500 Allied ships were destroyed and by the summer there were enough U-boats spread across the Atlantic to allow several wolf packs to attack numerous different convoy routes. The U-boats were running riot, following convoys by day and attacking them at night. In total over 1,600 ships were sunk in 1942, and Britain was starting to feel the pinch. Supplies of food and fuel were getting critically low and the local shipbuilders were struggling to keep up with the demand for replacement ships.

For a few months towards the end of 1942 it really was touch and go, but the development of new long-range aircraft such as B-24 Liberators meant that the Allies were now able to plug the 'Atlantic Gap', couple this with new anti-submarine weapons such as the *Hedgehog* (a large mortar fired from Royal Navy warships which detonated on contact with a U-boat) and life suddenly became much more dangerous for the U-boat crews. May 1943 was dubbed 'Black May' by the U-boat fleet; during that month forty-three U-boats were destroyed, thirty-four of which met their fate in the Atlantic. This was 25 per cent of their total numbers. Such a level of loss was simply unsustainable; gradually the U-boats were pulled out of the area to fight in other places. The Battle of the Atlantic had been lost.

The Merchant Navy lost over 3,500 vessels during the Battle of the Atlantic with over 36,000 merchant seamen killed. The Royal Navy lost 175 warships and thousands of crew. The Kriegsmarine lost 783 U-boats and approximately 30,000 submariners.

Turning Points in the Pacific: Coral Sea and Midway, 1942

By spring 1942 Japan was sitting pretty in Southeast Asia. After the devastation of Pearl Harbor they had managed to put all of the key areas of the region safely in their pocket and had set up a decent defensive barrier to protect their newly acquired assets.

There was no doubt that the attack on Pearl Harbor had severely dented America's ability to fight in the Pacific, however she had not been knocked out completely cold. Yes, she might have been dazed, surprised and a bit disorientated but she was still in the fight. And for Japan, that was bad news.

Shortly after Pearl Harbor, newly appointed Commander-in-Chief of the Pacific Fleet, Admiral Chester Nimitz, was given the unenviable job of holding a defensive line from Alaska to Midway in the Pacific, and then from Midway down to Australia. He had nowhere near enough vessels to accomplish this the 'traditional way' so, to use a business cliché, Nimitz was forced to 'think outside of the box' in order to form a successful defensive line across such a huge distance, so he got thinking... could he hold the line with air power?

While the Japanese basked in the glow of Pearl Harbor and set about conquering the rest of Southeast Asia, Nimitz quietly set about calling up his reserves and assembling and organising his fleet for battle. By the end of January 1942 he had managed to gather five aircraft carriers, sixteen cruisers, forty-four destroyers and sixteen submarines.

Not a bad little group to be honest.

In February Nimitz launched a few small-scale raids on Japanese positions on the Marshall Islands, Wake Island and Marcus Island. Although not much damage was done, it did bring the war alarmingly close to Tokyo, which in turn got Japanese nerves twitching. By April, Yamamoto had submitted plans for an attack on Midway, the official reason for the offensive was to gain control of the forward airfield on the eastern island of Midway and thus stop the Americans using it. But in reality, Yamamoto wanted to blow the US fleet out of the water once and for all.

As the Japanese top brass were mulling over Yamamoto's plan a US Air-Corps officer, Lieutenant-Colonel James Doolittle, was working on a plan of his own – a bombing raid on Tokyo launched from aircraft carriers. No one thought it was possible but on 18 April sixteen B-25s full to the brim with bombs set off for Tokyo, Nagoya, Osaka and Kobe. The Japanese public had been assured by their government that no enemy planes would ever reach their shores, so when the bombers roared in at a height barely above the treetops and dropped their bombs there was considerable panic amongst the civilian population as well as the Japanese government. Yamamoto had no problem getting his plan ratified.

Meanwhile, Japanese eyes were also turning to Australia. The use of Australia as a major Allied base was a very real possibility, so to nullify this threat the Japanese sent their 4th Fleet down to New Guinea to capture Port Moresby as well as Tulagi on the Solomon Islands. The problem here was that earlier in the year the clever backroom boys of the US Army had managed to crack the Japanese naval code. As a consequence, a US naval task force was immediately dispatched to intercept.

By 4 May, Japanese forces had successfully raised the *Rising Sun* flag over Tulagi, despite several supporting vessels being sunk or damaged by US aircraft from the USS *Yorktown*. Alerted that there were enemy warships in the vicinity, the Japanese fleet set course to track them down.

What became known as the Battle of Coral Sea marked something of a turning point in naval warfare. It was the first sea battle ever to be fought without a single salvo being fired from a warship. It was a sea battle without any sea battling. Instead the battle was fought by the big carriers and their aircraft. Over two days both sides exchanged carrier strikes, firstly the US sank the Japanese light carrier *Shōhō*, but they lost a destroyer and a fleet refueller vessel. The following day the two foes went at it again, this time the Japanese fleet carrier *Shōkaku* was heavily damaged, but the US lost its fleet carrier USS *Lexington* and suffered damage to the USS *Yorktown*. Both sides also lost countless aircraft and after day two the respective fleets retired to lick their wounds.

Technically, the Battle of Coral Sea was a tactical victory for the Japanese – they had inflicted more damage to more US ships than their enemy had managed to do to them. However, this was the first time the Japanese had not got their way in a fight – their advance had been halted, they had lost their shiny new 26,000-tonne carrier *Shōkaku,* and her sister carrier, the *Zuikaku,* had been left with virtually no operational aircraft. This meant that for the main assault on Midway they would find themselves significantly short of hardware.

The Japanese plan for victory at Midway was made up of three distinct sections. A forward force of submarines would lurk off of Pearl Harbor and report back on the size and shape of the US naval force they were going up against. Then they were to launch a diversionary attack on the Aleutian Islands (with the help of the Imperial Japanese Army), which they felt sure would force Nimitz to split his fleet and weaken his overall defence line. Once this had been achieved, they would then tease Nimitz to commit what was left of his force into an open sea battle by bombing Midway to bits. Yamamoto was confident that the losses suffered by the Americans at Coral Sea meant that he had the far superior fighting force and would be able to smash his enemy relatively easily.

The problem was that this plan was based on massive assumptions and also did not take into account that the Americans could listen in to what they were doing and knew pretty much every detail about their attack plan.

Consequently, Nimitz and his team knew that Midway was going to be invaded, but for security reasons they did not tell anyone stationed there that the greatest concentration of naval firepower ever assembled in the history of naval firepower was steaming at full chat directly to their little island. The garrison there was totally oblivious to what was about to kick off. Having said that, the island's anti-aircraft defences were reinforced and more patrol sorties were scheduled off the coast of the island, even though no one really knew what they were looking for.

By 2 June, Japanese forces were bearing down on the Aleutian Islands and over the next couple of days they succeeded in depositing a decent-sized land force on the island without too much trouble. However, the invasion failed to attract much interest from the Americans – they did not send any resources over to help, preferring to concentrate instead on what was going down at Midway. This was a huge strategic blow to Yamamoto's initial plan.

Meanwhile, by 3 June, the Japanese forward submarine group had arrived in Hawaii and had taken up their reconnaissance positions to spy on the US forces heading to Midway, however they were too late. US Task Force 16 had already left on 28 May, and US Task Force 17 had followed it into the Pacific forty-eight hours later. This left Yamamoto with no information on the size and scale of his enemy, he had little choice but to depend on his less than reliable intelligence service. It was another slap in the face for Yamamoto.

That same day a US Navy Catalina patrol plane spotted the Japanese invasion fleet approaching. It was 09:04hrs. Twenty-one minutes later another Catalina patrol spotted a large formation of enemy ships. Immediately the crew alerted their base. They were approximately 700 miles to the south west of Midway, technically within range of the American B-17 bombers based there, but local commanders wanted confirmation of the sighting before they were prepared to unleash the bombers. That confirmation came two hours later, once it had arrived the pilots of the B-17s were give the nod to get out there and smash 'em.

The Battle of Midway was on.

It took four hours for the B-17s to reach their target and due to the extra-large fuel tanks they had to enable them to fly so far, they were only able to carry four 500lb bombs each. None of them hit their target. Meanwhile, the news of the enemy formation found its way to the US carriers who were hanging about a few hundred miles northeast of Midway. Nimitz ordered carrier Task Force 16 and 17 to move south PDQ and prepare for an intercept.

By dawn the following day the Japanese fleet was just 280 miles from Midway. At 04:30hrs they launched 108 aircraft – their objective was to ruin the runways and destroy as many aircraft on the ground as possible. As they approached Midway and were picked up by the island's radar all available defensive aircraft were scrambled, including the B-17s so that they did not become sitting ducks. That said, seventeen defending aircraft were shot from the skies in that first attack – they were no match for the Japanese Zeros. Finding no planes on the ground to bomb, the enemy bombers smashed oil depots instead causing much damage. However as they returned to their carriers they had to admit that they had failed in meeting their primary objective. Even before the pilots of the first wave had returned, Admiral Nagumo was dishing out orders for a second attack.

It was at this time that US torpedo bombers from Midway arrived on the scene and had caught the Japanese carriers *Akagi* and *Kaga* at their most vulnerable as they were welcoming back their returning fighters. Numerous TBD Devastators attacked, but again they were no match for the Japanese fighters.

Undeterred, the lure of blowing two enemy aircraft carriers out of the water was too good an opportunity for the US Navy to miss, so plans were put in place to have another go. USS *Enterprise* and USS *Hornet* from Task Force 16 were sent forward to get closer to the enemy carrier fleet to enable their fighters to strike. USS *Yorktown* from Task Force 17 would follow on later. As they closed the gap, all three carriers launched their first wave of attacking aircraft. A total of 156 planes were on course to smash the enemy. Meanwhile the Japanese fleet was blissfully unaware that it had been found and what kind of force was about to hit it. Nagumo was busy getting ready for a second attack on Midway Island, confident that his position was secure. He had scout planes in the air too and none of them had reported back anything to worry him.

The trouble was, his reconnaissance was rubbish. Even though one of his scout planes flew right over Task Force 16 the pilot failed to notice anything. When something was eventually spotted and radioed in at 07:25hrs there was no mention of carriers in the report. Nagumo thought he was as safe as houses.

Then, just as the second wave of Zeros were about to launch for another go at Midway, Nagumo had a shock – one of his spotter planes had seen an enemy carrier. This was bad news indeed, but Nagumo also saw an opportunity. He cancelled the second wave of attacks on Midway, brought back his fleet defense fighters that had been circling and got everyone ready for a massive attack on the enemy fleet instead.

At 09:17hrs Nagumo had all of his planes ready to go and so turned his fleet around to head straight for his enemy. The decks of his ships were utter chaos as men rushed about desperately trying to rearm and refuel as many planes as possible for the attack. Little did they know (because none of the Japanese ships carried radar) that a squadron of torpedo bombers from the USS *Hornet* was just minutes away.

Things were about to get heavy.

Once again though, the TBD Devastators were no match for the Zeros that were quickly scrambled to defend the Japanese fleet. All fifteen torpedo bombers in the first wave were destroyed. Within minutes, more torpedo bombers from USS *Yorktown* and USS *Enterprise* joined in the fun but once more the Zeros took good care of them and not one Japanese ship was hit.

Once these torpedo bombers had been taken care of, Naguma once more prepared for his own attack. Just as the first of his strike force was about to take off a squadron of US dive-bombers roared down out of the clouds. It was 10:20hrs. The 38,200-tonne carrier *Kaga* was hit several times and was quickly transformed into a raging inferno, almost everyone on her bridge was killed.

As *Kaga* burned, the other carrier, *Akagi*, was launching the first plane en route to the American fleet. Just as that first plane took to the air, three US dive bombers attacked. The first bomb fell through the deck and exploded in one of the hangars below, subsequent bombs fell among the waiting aircraft on deck – fuel and bombs quickly ignited, killing some of the best pilots Japan had to offer.

Next on the dive bombers' hit list was the 18,800-ton carrier *Soryu*. In just a matter of minutes the most powerful carrier force on the water had been smashed to bits. Only the 20,000-ton *Hiryu* remained operational and the order immediately went up for her to let loose her strike force – there was still a slim chance that a devastating blow could be delivered to the enemy.

The USS *Yorktown* was the target, but by the time the first wave of Japanese planes got to within striking distance there was already a formidable welcome party waiting. Twelve of the initial eighteen Japanese attackers were blown out of the sky, that said, the USS *Yorktown* was hit three times by bombs and, after a second wave added a few torpedoes into the mix, the *Yorktown* was listing so badly that the order was given to abandon ship.

As the crew of the USS *Yorktown* were leaving the ship, news arrived that *Hiryu* had been spotted, she was only 100 miles northwest of the stricken *Yorktown*. At 15:30hrs the USS *Enterprise* launched twenty-five Dauntless dive bombers and the USS *Hornet* launched another sixteen – their sole objective was to destroy the *Hiryu*. At 17:05hrs the bombers screamed down on the unsuspecting *Hiryu* and hit her with four bombs, transforming her into a floating fireball.

The last remaining Japanese carrier was finished. On 5 June Yamamoto realised he had nowhere to go and called off the attack on Midway. He had lost all four of his aircraft carriers, one heavy cruiser, over 300 aircraft and 3,500 men killed. In contrast, the US had lost one carrier, one destroyer, 147 aircraft and 307 men.

Midway was a shattering defeat for Japan, she struggled to replace the planes, pilots and carriers lost in the battle and as a consequence found herself always playing 'catch-up' with America. In the time it took Japan to build three new carriers, the US churned out dozens of new ships.

The balance of power in the Pacific had changed hands for good.

Sun, Sand and Semi-automatics: North Africa, 1942

After Wavell's successful counterattack against the Italians, the British had captured an area the size of England and France combined. It was an incredible victory and did much to raise morale back home where hundreds of thousands of people were still being bombed daily by the Luftwaffe. For Mussolini, it was a serious set back to his plan, as well as a significant dent to his ego.

For the British, Tripoli (the capital of Libya) was now in sight, but then Churchill removed a large chunk of the desert force to help out in Greece. An opportunity had been lost to push the Axis out of Africa.

Meanwhile, Hitler and his chums had been busy figuring out a way of helping the Italians out in Africa. On 12 February 1941 a detachment of men and machines set sail for Tripoli, they would soon become one of the most famous fighting units of the war. Initially the remit of this small army was to occupy as many British troops as possible and to act as a defensive cover for the southern flank of the Third Reich. In the end they were to do much, much more than just hold their positions and annoy the British. These men were the Afrika Korps.

The man Hitler had chosen to help dig Mussolini out of his hole in the sand had already worked wonders in France in 1940. His name was Erwin Rommel. Although he knew nothing about desert warfare he was bold, aggressive and a quick learner and as soon as his men landed in Tripoli they were marched straight into the frontline. On 24 March, even though some of his men were still waiting to disembark from their troop ships, Rommel went on the attack, quickly defeating the British at El Agheila and once more at Mersa el Brega on 31 March. By 15 April, the British had been pushed back 500 miles all the way through Libya and back to the Egyptian town of Solum. The British Eighth Army was in full retreat, with the Germans taking prisoners by the thousands including General Sir Richard O'Connor, Commander of the Allied Western Desert Force and

Churchill's top man in Africa. Only Tobruk had managed to avoid Rommel's clutches.

Tobruk was a vital sea port and as such was coveted by both sides. Rommel desperately wanted it to help ease the burden on his supply lines, which were now stretched across the whole of Libya. Without Tobruk, he couldn't really go much further into Egypt. The Allies knew this of course and were not about to give the city up without a fight. Frustrated that Tobruk had not been captured during his advance Rommel decided to smash the city's defences to pieces and while his artillery guns were put into position, he made a few calls to his mates in the Luftwaffe. It was time for Tobruk to get 'Blitz'd'.

Over a thousand raids were mounted against Tobruk. The Royal Navy brought in fresh supplies and more defenders to help hold the city, at the same time as they were operating from Malta they were able to seriously mess with Rommel's own supply lines into Tripoli. As a consequence the Afrika Korps started to suffer serious shortages of supplies, especially fuel for their panzers. Without this fuel they had no hope of pushing further into Egypt. This was a blow, as was the fact that regardless of how hard he knocked, Rommel could not open the door to Tobruk.

#frustrating

For the time being, the war in desert was at a stalemate.

Churchill was also getting a bit fed up with the lack of action in the desert and urged his new commander (appointed in July), General Claude Auchinleck, to launch an attack and give Rommel a hiding. Operation *Crusader* was drawn up with the idea of destroying the enemy's armoured forces, then sending the infantry in to finish off the job. Not only would a successful attack relieve the pressure on Tobruk, but it also might just push the Afrika Korps all they way back to Libya. Operation *Crusader* kicked off on 18 November 1941, but it did not go very well. German panzers were better than the British tanks, and the German big anti-tank guns were way better than anything Auchinleck had in his arsenal. General Alan Cunningham, who was leading the attack, strongly suggested to Auchinleck that the offensive be cancelled. After careful consideration Auchinleck sacked Cunningham and appointed Major General Neil Ritchie. The attack would continue.

On paper, the decision to continue the fight was madness. The Afrika Korps were running riot and from an outsider's perspective, it seemed that the Allied forces were looking squarely down the barrel of defeat. But the panzers were running out fuel. They just couldn't keep up the pressure and were eventually forced to fall back. By Christmas 1941, Rommel had retreated 500 miles and was back where he had started. Tobruk had been saved and now it was the Allies' turn to push the Nazis out of Africa for good.

Except it wasn't.

Yet again, when the opportunity for a decisive victory was within touching distance, troops were whisked away from Africa to fight the good fight somewhere else. This time it was the Far East as Japan's entry into the war threatened British interests in Burma and Malaya.

It was yet another opportunity lost, and to make matters worse, within a few weeks Rommel counter- attacked. Big time. Struggling with their own supply issues and the loss of men and machines to Asia, the Allied forces were considerably weakened and Rommel was able to push forward rapidly. By February, his panzers were once again within spitting distance of Tobruk. Richie laid out a defensive wall of mines and fortifications in front of Tobruk facing west, however Rommel simply moved his forces south and went round the side and attacked from the rear. He now had a free run at Tobruk.

Tobruk had taken a beating over the last nine months or so and its defenses were not in the best of shape. Added to which, the Royal Navy could no longer guarantee delivery of supplies and reinforcements and it was plain to see that the city would struggle to cope with another sustained assault. That assault materialised on 20 June 1941 and it was an absolute humdinger. Rommel threw everything he had at the southern defenses of Tobruk, this time the defenders had no chance. Twenty-four hours later, a triumphant Rommel received the formal surrender of Tobruk and its garrison of 34,000 men. Hitler was delighted and immediately promoted Rommel to the rank of Field Marshal. The men of the Afrika Korps were delighted too; the garrison of Tobruk yielded a massive haul of booty in the form of fuel, rations and transport – all fundamental to the continuation of the fight. Churchill, however, was not impressed. Not only did he have to suffer the embarrassment of finding out the news in front of President Roosevelt, but also back home in London pressure was mounting on him to deliver some kind of victory. The press were rabid in their criticism, calling for a full enquiry into the handling of the war in Africa, hailing the whole thing an utter disaster.

Back in the desert, the British continued to fall back; they were in full retreat and in utter chaos. The retirement continued deep into Egypt until on 30 June 1942 they reached a railway halt just sixty miles from Alexandria.

El Alamein.

The End of the Beginning: El Alamein, 1942

It was not by chance that Auchinleck decided that El Alamein would be the place where his men would stop running and fight. This little patch of North African desert was unlike any other in the area. Yes, the sea was still to the north, but just forty miles inland there was another sea, not of water but of salt marshes. The Qattara Depression was huge and completely impassable for tanks and other motorised armour. It could technically be outflanked to the south, but that would mean crossing into the Sahara Desert and that too was almost impossible terrain for a tank.

The fighting at El Alamein would be different. There could be no flanking or outmanoeuvring, no diving round the sides; this would be a full frontal war of attrition. Auchinleck told his men to dig in and prepare for the final battle for North Africa.

Rommel moved up to El Alamein on 30 June, his men were tired and once again supply lines were stretched to breaking point, but sitting back and waiting was not Rommel's style, and no sooner than had he arrived in the area his Afrika Korps were on the attack in one final desperate attempt to kick the British out of Africa. For the Allies it was touch and go, the Afrika Korps threatened to break through, but RAF air superiority in the flat, coverless desert proved to be decisive. Enemy armoured formations had nowhere to hide and soon Rommel was down to just thirty-seven tanks and his attack petered out.

In August Churchill visited Cairo to see for himself what was going on. He was desperate for a victory and kept urging his commanders to attack, attack, attack. Auchinleck wanted to wait until September, which would give him time to rest and reinforce his men and properly plan the attack. Churchill, however, wasn't going to hang about and placed a new man in charge of the Eighth Army – Field Marshal Bernard Law Montgomery – despite him never setting foot in the desert before.

Meanwhile Rommel was busy scratching his head trying to figure out how he could achieve a breakthrough. He wasn't in a great position if we are being honest, not only were his men on the brink of exhaustion but his old friend Hitler had eyes only for the Russian front. As a consequence his Führer was unable (or unwilling) to guarantee the supplies coming into Tripoli and with the RAF and Royal Navy in control of the local waters, deploying from their bases in Malta, only 25 per cent of German supply ships managed to reach their destination.

Belatedly, the German High Command agreed to try and destroy these bases on Malta. The Luftwaffe was given free rein to smash the island to pieces. Day after day the raids came; Malta became the most bombed place on the planet, but the island held out. Just.

The defiance of Malta was a blow to Rommel as it meant that the Allies continued to enjoy air superiority in the desert. It was a vital tactical advantage. It also meant that Rommel still had to contend with supply lines that were almost 1,500 miles long. Every day thousands of trucks ran the gauntlet to and from Tripoli and Bengazi fetching much needed supplies, and every day the RAF had fun trying to blow these trucks off the road. In contrast, the British supply lines were just sixty miles long.

Montgomery quickly got busy hatching a plan. He knew that Rommel would not be able to outflank him this time due to the Qattara Depression, so he ordered his tanks to dig in and take up defensive positions. He did not want to be suckered into a counterattack.

Monty expected the Germans to attack during the full moon of 26 August, but the attack never happened. In the meantime, Monty and his mates decided to have a game with the Germans – they mocked up a map of the British defences which gave a highly detailed (but very inaccurate) picture of the Allied minefields and defensive positions and then they 'lost' the papers after an armoured car had 'broken down' in No Man's Land.

The Germans took the bait and when they did finally attack at dawn on 31 August, the progress of the forward panzer force was very slow. They kept running into minefields where they did not expect them to be and the Allied artillery was strangely accurate. Not surprisingly after taking a bit of a tonking, Rommel called off the attack on 3 September.

It was round one to Monty and he hadn't even laced his gloves up yet.

As August made way for September, the Allies started to receive hundreds of shiny new Sherman tanks and self-propelled guns from America – a gift from Roosevelt to help them recapture Tobruk. Churchill kept enquiring as to when the offensive would be launched, but Montgomery was not a man to be rushed. Any advance would not be until October. In the meantime he went to great lengths to disguise what he planned to do in an effort to fool his enemy. Traditionally, the Eighth Army had always attacked from the south, trying to drive the enemy into the sea. Monty guessed that Rommel would expect a similar kind of assault and as such planned to do exactly the opposite. He would attack from the north. But, to keep Rommel and his cronies guessing, Monty put in place a huge deception plan that included thousands of dummy tanks and a fake fuel pipeline. Fake radio traffic all contributed to the Axis thinking that the attack was planned for November and would, as usual, come from the south.

Meanwhile the Germans were doing some planning and preparation of their own. Due to a smaller battlefield, a shortage of fuel and a lack of equipment, Rommel was forced to devise deep defensive positions behind a monster minefield made up of half a million mines. Dubbed 'The Devil's Garden' by the Germans it was a formidable defensive belt up to five miles deep in places. With no option to go round the sides, Rommel knew that if the Allies wanted to attack, they would have to attack through his minefield.

By mid-October Montgomery was ready. The advance would be dubbed Operation *Lightfoot* (no doubt a tongue-in-cheek reference to the massive

German minefield they had to cross) and would involve 195,000 men and just over 1,000 tanks. On the other side of the minefield the Afrika Korps had been bolstered to 116,000 men and almost 550 tanks. However there was one person missing: Rommel. The strain of the fight had become too much for the German field marshal and he had fallen ill and was back in Germany resting up.

Monty's plan was simple. Pull together a huge number of big artillery guns, point them at the Germans and let them have it big style. Meanwhile, while the enemy had their heads well and truly down, large numbers of infantry were sent forward to clear a path through the minefield (easier said than done in the middle of a monumental barrage). Once a safe path had been cleared it would be time for the tanks to do their thing.

These were not tactics of finesse or flamboyancy. This would be a battle of attrition, a throwback to how war was fought twenty-five years previous. It would be a First World War battle fought with Second World War weapons.

During the afternoon of 23 October 1942 Montgomery gave the nod for his tanks and guns to move up into their final positions. At 21.40hrs local time, the guns let rip. One thousand guns opened fire from the Mediterranean coast to the Qattara Depression and continued to smash the German positions to bits for over six hours. Meanwhile, thousands of Allied sappers crept forwards to clear a path – just wide enough for one tank – through the minefield. Using mine detectors, specially adapted tanks and the good ol' bayonet, they painstakingly set about their work with the infantry and tanks following closely behind.

The attack took the Germans completely by surprise. Rommel was still in Germany, but not for long. Upon hearing of the Allied offensive he immediately returned to the desert where he set about organising a counterattack. He was annoyed that his panzers had not been let loose on the Allies while they were still bogged down in the minefield. Now it was too late, the window of opportunity had closed, the counterattack failed and resulted in losses he could ill afford.

Saying that, it was not all fun and games for the Allies. The paths through the minefields were treacherous and if a single tank broke down or was adversely affected by the sand a massive column of transport was stuck behind it with no hope of going around the stricken vehicle. They were all sitting ducks, especially to the impressive 88mm German anti-tank guns which had a field day knocking out stranded Allied tanks and other vehicles stuck in the minefields. In an effort to improve the situation Montgomery called in the RAF who flew 1,000 sorties over the next couple of days dropping 135 tonnes of explosives on the Axis defenders.

Despite all of this, the breakthrough did not come.

By the end of October, Rommel was in a precarious position but was still managing to hold his line, although he was using up a lot of his reserves. The main attack from the Allies had by now petered out, with Montgomery withdrawing some of his men back into his reserves, which irritated Churchill no end. The PM wanted a victory. He *needed* a victory. What was Montgomery doing withdrawing men instead of crushing the enemy?

What Montgomery was doing was setting himself up for the final push, which would place the Eighth Army on the road to Tunis.

Operation *Supercharge*.

The plan for Operation *Supercharge* was practically identical to that of Operation *Lightfoot*. A massive artillery bombardment with sappers clearing a path through the rest of the minefield that would allow the tanks to get through and force a fight out in the open.

Supercharge opened up with a seven-hour air bombardment on German positions and supply centres, followed by a four-hour artillery assault with

360 guns firing over 15,000 rounds. The assaulting troops, led by Major-General Freyberg's New Zealand Division, commenced their advance at 01.05hrs on 2 November. This time progress through the minefield was much better and soon there were numerous tank battles taking place at very close range. The next forty-eight hours would see the biggest tank battle of the desert war. The battlefield was a killing zone and the Allies were taking huge losses, however they had the advantage of vastly superior numbers and by crudely smashing and smashing at the German lines they gradually wore the Afrika Korps down. By 3 November Rommel could count just thirty-five tanks left.

For Rommel, the time had come to get out of there and retreat. He put a call in to Hitler to explain the situation. Hitler was not having any of it. Retreat was out of the question. Then, the RAF dropped another 400 tonnes of bombs on to the heads of the Afrika Korps, this time Rommel was not in the mood to ask permission. It was time to save what he could and get out.

The German lines were breached on 4 November with the Germans in full retreat. However torrential rain meant that the Eighth Army could not continue the chase – the opportunity to completely destroy Rommel's army had disappeared.

That said, the Battle of El Alamein was over and had ended in a much-needed victory for the Allies. Montgomery had shown that Rommel could be beaten, that the Nazis were not unstoppable and that the Axis rule in the desert could be broken.

Churchill had his victory. A delighted Prime Minister spoke at the Lord Mayor's Day luncheon in London on 10 November telling the gathered crowd that this: *'...is not the end. It is not even the beginning of the end. But it is, perhaps, the end of the beginning.'*

There was still much work to be done to kick the Axis out of the desert for good. On 8 November an Anglo-American force landed in North Africa with the aim of seizing control of the ports of Casablanca, Oran and Algiers and then squashing Rommel between the two armies. Commanding the invasion force was an obscure American officer who had never seen action, let alone managed a full-on seaborne landing.

His name was Dwight D. Eisenhower.

A Taste of Things to Come: Operation *Torch*, 1942

Ever since Hitler had started banging on his door in June 1941, Stalin had been urging Churchill to open up a new fighting front in an effort to relieve the pressure on Mother Russia. The thing was, Churchill did not fancy another tear up in France any time soon – his army simply wasn't strong enough. Despite a full-scale invasion of mainland Europe being out of the question until at least 1943, it was agreed between the Allied bigwigs that the experimental 'mini invasion' of Dieppe, which had been in planning for a while already, could still go ahead. These small-scale landings would be led by Lord Louis Mountbatten and were designed to indicate whether a full-blown invasion of Europe was feasible or not.

The Dieppe raid was pencilled in for 19 August 1942. It was an unmitigated disaster. Out of the 6,000 men who took part in the landings 4,384 were killed, wounded or missing – a staggering 73 per cent. All the equipment landed on shore was lost. On top of that, the Royal Navy lost 550 men and thirty-four ships. The RAF, in what was the largest single-day air battle of the war, flew 2,617 sorties and lost 106 planes; Wehrmacht casualties were 591.

The mistakes of the Dieppe raid were many. It proved that a full frontal seaborne invasion against a heavily defended coastline could not be successful without prior bombing from both sea and air and without significant reconnaissance patrols. It was a hard and costly lesson, but ultimately would prove vital in the successful planning of Operation *Overlord*.

Back in Moscow, Stalin was less than impressed with the whole Dieppe show. He wanted a second front opened and he was running out of patience. Churchill and Roosevelt needed to come up with something a bit better. Quickly.

The recent victory at El Alamein provided the opportunity for a second front to be opened in the south. If the Allies could control North Africa, they could then use it as a launch pad to get to Sicily. From there they could jump across to mainland Italy and move up the so-called 'soft underbelly' of Europe. Such a move would also help clear the Mediterranean of enemy naval activity.

Following Montgomery's success in the desert, large chunks of North Africa were in the hands of the Allies, however there was a decent portion of the area that was run by Vichy France (a puppet government of Nazi Germany headed up by Marshal Phillipe Pétain). If they could overrun these territories it would effectively squeeze the Afrika Korps out of the area for good and leave the path open for a journey north into Europe.

From a PR point of view it was agreed that, despite the operation (codenamed 'Torch') being a joint Anglo-American gig with, in fact, more British troops taking part than American, it should appear to be an American show. Planning for the invasion was placed on the desk of a relatively unknown American officer called Dwight D. Eisenhower and on the ground the top man would be another American: Major-General George C. Patton.

The key to Operation *Torch*'s success would be a successful amphibious landing and Eisenhower had earmarked over 60,000 men to come ashore via three separate landing sites: A Western Taskforce of 35,000 men would come directly from the USA to land at Casablanca on the Moroccan Atlantic Coast; a Centre Taskforce of 18,500 men including the 1st US Armored Division would land near Oran in western Algeria; and an Eastern Taskforce made up of 20,000 men including two British Commando units would land near Algiers, more than 250 miles to the east in Algeria. Once the landings had taken place the invasion force would head inland towards Tunisia, some 500 miles away.

It was big, brash and ambitious. Nothing like this had ever been attempted before.

Facing these 60,000 plus invaders would be 125,000 soldiers of Vichy France, but they didn't have the best equipment at their disposal and Allied intelligence seemed to suggest that they wouldn't put up too much of a fight. The landings would take place on 8 November 1942.

There were no preliminary air or naval bombardments before the men attempted to get ashore as the hope was that the French soldiers based in and around the landing zones would not resist the landings. This was one of the reasons why the whole invasion was portrayed as an American affair as it was thought that the French might react better to the Americans than the British. Some British infantrymen even wore US Army uniforms for the landings.

Overall the initial landings were a success with only minimal resistance. By the afternoon of 8 November Admiral Darlan, the leader of the Vichy French troops in the area, recognised that his men were in a hopeless decision and quickly agreed to a ceasefire in Algiers. Forty-eight hours later the ceasefire was in place for the whole of French North Africa. That same day Patton pocketed the keys to Casablanca.

After mopping up the immediate areas around the invasion zones, the Allied troops consolidated and pushed on towards Tunisia, some 500 miles distant. However, on hearing of the invasion, Hitler moved quickly to reinforce the area around Tunis with fresh German and Italian troops. By 20 November the advance slowed down, the momentum had gone and the Axis defenders had dug themselves in well – they were not going to be shifted quickly.

Despite this slight disappointment, Operation *Torch* was a success. French North Africa had been occupied and a major amphibious landing / invasion had taken place. It would prove vital experience for what was to come.

Not One Step Back: Stalingrad, 1942

Hitler may not have liked to hear it, but Operation *Barbarossa* had failed. On the Eastern Front the winter of 1941–42 had been appalling. Without proper clothing and equipment, and constantly being hounded by Zhukov's Russian forces, morale was at an all-time low. Repeated requests by generals to retreat to warmer and safer areas were continually refused, yet, somehow – despite the misery, despite the hardships, despite the casualties – those German soldiers held their line. It was, without doubt, a remarkable achievement.

Hitler was suitably impressed, so much so, that by April 1942 he was feeling brave enough to issue *Führer Directive No. 41* which laid out plans for a summer offensive in the East. However, the disaster of the first attempt on Russia had left his eastern army severely depleted. The Wehrmacht had lost nigh-on a million men in the East already and there was no hope of putting on a coordinated attack across the whole of the front. Instead Hitler chose to concentrate on the south, specifically he wanted to take control of the vast oil reserves that were hiding down in the Caucasus.

The plan was simple: drive east towards Stalingrad and in the process encircle the main bulk of Russian forces. Then, with the Russians trapped, a second fighting force would head south, through the town of Rostov and on to the oil fields. The mighty Sixth Army, under the leadership of General Paulus, would head to Stalingrad, their objectives were to eradicate the industrial capability of the city and take control of the River Volga – a vital communications route south to the Caucasus. While they were busy with that little job, the First and Fourth Panzer Armies under Colonel-Generals von Klest and Hoth respectively would make a beeline for the oil fields.

The initial advance was rapid; in fact many of the advancing German Army saw only glimpses of the enemy as they continually melted away from the advance. Many Germans thought that the Russian Red Army was broken and that victory was a mere formality – a premise that was substantially backed up on 23 July when Rostov was occupied. With Rostov captured the oil fields were now at Hitler's mercy, as a consequence he made the trek down to the south the priority. Forward detachments of the Sixth Army were just a hundred miles away from Stalingrad – this was just too easy.

Only, it wasn't. The Germans may have taken Rostov, but the fighting was intense and although Soviet losses were significant, the bulk of the Red Army based in the city were able to escape without being taken prisoner. They lived to fight again. Also, in Hitler's eagerness to get his hands on all of that lovely oil in the Caucasus region, the Sixth Army was stripped of much of its fuel and almost all of its panzers, so they could add to the push south. This hampered the progress towards Stalingrad, but by 23 August forward units of the Sixth Army reached the western bank of the River Volga towards the northern suburbs of Stalingrad. That evening 600 Luftwaffe bombers dished out substantial punishment to key industrial areas of the city.

The Battle of Stalingrad had begun.

Stalingrad was an important city for Russia. Situated on the border between European and Asian Russia, it was a key centre of industry, manufacturing and trade, and not surprisingly it was also a vital communications hub with an extensive rail network as well as the mighty River Volga running through the city. It was a model city of the Russian ideal and one that they were intensely proud of, so much so that it was renamed after their illustrious leader. Because of all this, it would not be given up lightly. If the Germans wanted to get their hands on Stalingrad, they had better be prepared to fight for it.

Hitler did want it. Badly. Not because of any overarching strategic imperative, the main point of this whole advance into the south of Russia was to capture the oil, but because he thought he could take it. OK, controlling Stalingrad would control access to the Volga and with that there was a vital transport link to and from the oil fields, but most importantly, smashing up Stalingrad would be a massive boost to Hitler's ego and a crushing blow to Stalin.

It all started off swimmingly for Hitler, the initial bombing raids were backed up by heavy artillery bombardments and caused panic and widespread devastation. More than 40,000 civilians were killed and vast areas of the city were quickly reduced to piles of rubble.

But the city was not destroyed.

The Nazi air Blitzkrieg had ultimately failed to deliver a quick surrender of Stalingrad. The massive bombing attack had ruined, but not completely destroyed, the city and it was still fighting back. It was time to send in the tanks.

When Paulus gave the nod to his men to start the ground advance he promised Hitler that Stalingrad would be his by the end of September. They were both going to be bitterly disappointed. Back in 1941, in the early days of Operation *Barbarossa*, the German panzers had performed brilliantly. In the wide, open plains of rural Russia they dominated the battlefields and brushed aside all attempts at defense.

In Stalingrad, however, it would be slightly different.

The tanks that had performed so well out in the open struggled in the relative confines of the city. Rubble blocked many streets and thoroughfares and made progress difficult and slow. In addition, the thousands of bombed out buildings that still stood provided the defending Red Army perfect opportunities to build traps, strongpoints and fortified positions. Slow moving tanks were easy targets, especially if the attackers were high up on the upper floors of the buildings. Not only could they easily surprise their attackers with some welcoming explosives, but also the tanks were not designed to fire high into the air, so they struggled to return fire.

If that wasn't bad enough, the city was quickly infested with millions of rats that took a great liking to the canvas-covered wiring systems of the tanks – hundreds of them suffered electrical failures at the hands (or teeth) of Red Army rodents.

Every day throughout September the Stuka dive bombers attacked the city. Every day throughout September the artillery shells rained down to smash yet more buildings. At the beginning of October Paulus was ordered to take the city at any cost and on 7 October he launched a huge attack with two divisions. It was a complete and utter disaster. Almost four battalions were destroyed and scores of tanks were lost. It became very clear very quickly that the Sixth Army could not count on their armour to spearhead their attack. If Paulus was to take the city, the job would have to be done by the good old German infantryman. By the end of the month Paulus had over 100,000 men inside the city dishing it out to the Red Army, but, while Hitler was demanding the city be taken at any cost, Stalin was equally demanding that the city should be held at any cost. Each night the Red Army received reinforcements via ferry boats from the other side of the Volga. For the Germans inside the city it seemed that as soon as they killed ten Russian soldiers, another twenty appeared in their place.

Russian Commanders knew that in a fair fight they had no chance against the highly trained members of the German Wehrmacht. They had to find something that could somehow turn the fight to their advantage. That thing was home advantage – an intimate knowledge of the city they were in. They turned ruined buildings into fortified positions on every corner; they connected them with trenches, sometimes even using the sewer system under the city as a way of moving about undetected. They sheltered in basements converted in to bunkers and laid booby traps at every possible opportunity. Any kind of advance made by the Germans was slow and very costly.

On 14 October Hitler issued one of his directives, ordering all troops on the Eastern Front (apart from those at Stalingrad and on their way to the Caucasus) to stop fighting and dig in for winter. He was convinced that the Russians would not be able to do anything over the winter; he would sit it out and smash them to bits in the spring.

Unfortunately for Hitler, Stalin and Zhukov were very much planning to have a fight that winter and were at that very moment conjuring up the mother of all counterattacks in an attempt to cut off and encircle the Axis forces in Stalingrad. On 19 November over 1 million men, backed up by over 13,500 guns, almost 900 tanks and over 1,000 aircraft were primed to attack two positions simultaneously north and south of the German Sixth Army, some sixty miles west of Stalingrad. These areas of the Axis line were held, not by elite Wehrmacht troops, but by Rumanians.

The first attack was to the north, despite fighting vigorously the Russian 5th Tank Army bulldozed its way through the line, practically annihilating the Rumanian 1st Armoured Division as it did so. Back in Germany Hitler didn't really know what was going on, but during the evening of the 19th he ordered Paulus to sort something out and deal with the breach in the line in the north. Little did he know that the following morning would see something even bigger go down in the south.

At 10:00hrs the following morning a huge artillery bombardment commenced to the south of Stalingrad, this time the Rumanians didn't put up any kind of fight and very quickly surrendered. By the 23rd the Russian forces from the northern and southern attacks joined up at the village of Sovetsky, thus completely cutting off the Axis forces in Stalingrad.

For Paulus, this was a nightmare situation. He was encircled and cut off from the rest of the Wehrmacht with his ammunition and food supplies running low. The only viable option now open to him was to try and fight out of the encirclement but Hitler was adamant that Paulus should hold on to Stalingrad, whatever the cost; the Luftwaffe would drop supplies to his beleaguered troops from the air.

Göring had promised that his Luftwaffe would be able to drop 500 tonnes of supplies a day into Stalingrad. However, in the beginning they managed less than 100 tonnes a day, rising slightly in the second half of December to an average of 135 tonnes a day. This level fell once more as the weather worsened. To rub salt into the wound, Göring lost almost 500 aircraft during seventy days trying to supply Paulus.

During November the Germans tried to break back into Stalingrad in order to rescue Paulus and the 270,000-odd men that were trapped. They got close, very close (within thirty miles of the city), but ultimately failed due to another monstrous Russian counterattack, which would take them south towards Rostov. The attempt to relieve Stalingrad was over. Meanwhile the Russians continued south towards Rostov, forcing the Luftwaffe to move their bases further out the way, making air drops in Stalingrad even more difficult.

Within Stalingrad, Paulus and his men were starving, freezing and without fuel or ammunition. On 8 January, the Red Army offered a ceasefire in return for a full German surrender. Paulus refused to answer, so the Russians fired up 7,000 artillery guns and smashed the German positions to bits once more. On 26 January the Russians split the Sixth Army into two – that was the final straw. On 30 January Paulus informed Hitler that the situation was untenable and his men were hours from collapse. Hitler responded by promoting many of the officers on the ground in an effort to boost their morale and give them the impetus to hold on to what they had. Significantly Hitler promoted Paulus to the rank of Field Marshal, knowing that no Prussian or German field marshal had ever surrendered on the field of battle. The message was clear: Hitler expected Paulus to die fighting or to commit suicide.

The newly appointed field marshal did neither – instead he surrendered on 31 January.

Stalingrad was one of the most deadly battles in the history of deadly battles; almost 2 million men became casualties (killed / wounded / captured). It also signalled a distinct turning point in the war. Before Stalingrad, the German Army had known nothing but victory, after Stalingrad, they would know nothing but defeat.

Getting Grisly in the South Pacific: Guadalcanal, 1942–43

Despite the setback at Midway, the Japanese continued with their grand plan of generally annoying the Americans in the South Pacific by occupying a string of small islands at the southern end of the Solomons, in and around New Guinea. In particular they had their eyes on the island of Tulagi, which they wanted to use as a small naval base, and the island of Guadalcanal. By August 1942 the Japanese were sitting pretty on both islands, they were particularly comfortable at Guadalcanal where they had about 8,400 men and a fully functioning airfield at Lunga Point, complete with a significant artillery defence built into the surrounding hills. Such Japanese presence in the South Solomon Islands pushed them dangerously close to important sea routes between America and Australia, and so the Americans became rather twitchy about the whole situation.

Allied intelligence in the area was very good and the Americans knew well what the Japanese were up to, and started to plan accordingly. By August they themselves were ready for a pre-emptive attack on both Guadalcanal and Tulagi in an effort to kick the Japanese out of the South Solomon Islands and relieve the pressure on their supply lines.

On 7 August 1942, under the watchful gaze of Major General Alexander Vandegrift, 19,000 men of the 1st US Marine Division landed across both islands. The airstrip on Guadalcanal was taken without much of a fight and 2,000 Japanese defenders retired swiftly into the jungle. Within two days the important port at Tulagi was also in American hands. Awesome.

Not so awesome for the Japanese though, who were really fed up with the whole situation and immediately sent a naval task force of seven battlecruisers to sort it all out. They arrived on the scene during the night of 8/9 August and immediately set about the US Navy contingent anchored just off of Tulagi, sinking four US cruisers and damaging another two – causing the rest of the US fleet to retreat.

An additional 900 Japanese men were soon landed on the island, some twenty miles from the captured airfield, there were another 1,200 men on their way as back-up but the top Japanese officer on the ground, a Colonel Kiyonao Ichiki was not in the mood to hang about and wait. He immediately marched his men through thick jungle straight for the Americans who were about to discover that capturing the airfield was going to be a lot easier than holding on to it.

On 18 August a Japanese advance party encroached a little bit too far forward and was all but wiped out. Alerted to the impending danger the Americans quickly sorted themselves out, by the evening of 20 August, the American forces were dug in with artillery and machine-gun support along the west bank of Alligator Creek – a saltwater lagoon separated from the sea by a narrow sandbank about fifteen metres wide and thirty metres long. They lay ready and waiting for whatever the Japanese were going to throw at them.

In the early hours of 21 August the Japanese attacked. It was all about to get grisly on Guadalcanal.

Just after midnight Ichiki's men arrived on the east bank of the creek. An hour or so later they hit the American lines on the opposite bank with mortar fire, then about 100 Japanese soldiers dashed across the sandbank to get at the Americans. The majority of the attackers were cut to pieces by machine-gun fire, but a handful did manage to get across and actually inside the American positions, although any kind of success was shortlived and only a few of the men from that first wave survived.

Undeterred, at 02:30hrs Ichiki had another go at the American lines: 150 to 200 Japanese troops once more attacked across the sandbar and once more were almost completely wiped out. The sandbank was reminiscent of a First World War battlefield – completely covered with the dead and the dying, but Ichiki was unmoved and after a short, sharp mortar fight, he sent another wave of men across at about 05:00hrs. This time they tried to outflank the Americans by wading out to sea and attacking up the beach behind the west bank, they were met with devastating machine-gun and artillery fire forcing them to abandon their attack and retreat back to the east bank of the creek.

Out of the 917 Imperial soldiers who attacked across the sandbank that night, only 128 survived.

Over the coming weeks the Japanese Imperial Army continued to reinforce the island by night. Because of the dangers posed to the Imperial fleet from American planes operating out of the captured airfield, they could only use warships to drop men off, these warships (typically light destroyers) could make the trip under the cover of darkness, but were not able to carry all of the heavy equipment the infantry needed on the ground – such as vehicles, artillery and extra rations. Despite this, and despite another failed attempt on the airfield, by mid-October the opposing infantry were roughly equal in size with 22,000 Japanese and 23,000 Americans.

Things really started hotting up in October with the Japanese launching a number of heavy attacks on the American-held airfield, even the Imperial Navy got in on the fun, bombarding the area and taking out a couple of small American ships. On 26 October there was a more meaningful naval fight that led to the sinking of the US carrier *Hornet* although the Japanese also suffered significant damage to two carriers and lost a large number of skilled aircrew – something they would never fully recover from.

The American forces once more managed to halt the Imperial Army before they got their hands on the vital airfield, yet all was not rosy in the US garden. They were not making any territorial progress themselves and were unable to stop the Japanese reinforcements that were coming onto the island almost daily. By mid-November the balance of infantry numbers on the island tipped towards the Japanese for the first time; something had to be done to stop the Japanese overrunning the island.

Enter the US Navy.

In early November the Japanese attempted to put 7,000 men on shore using a large convoy of troop ships heavily supported by destroyers. They arrived at Ironbottom Sound, just off the Guadalcanal coast, during the night of 12/13 November, but due to good intelligence the US Navy was waiting for them. A fierce naval firefight kicked off which left six US ships and three Japanese vessels (including a battleship) at the bottom of the sea. The next day American aircraft attacked the Japanese landing fleet, sinking a cruiser and seven troop transport ships. Another naval scrap took place during the night of 14/15 November in the same place, the Japanese lost another battleship and a destroyer while the US lost three destroyers. The result of all this was that only about 2,000 men managed to get ashore and were unable to land any military supplies.

The Imperial Navy had one more go at getting to Guadalcanal on 30 November when Rear Admiral Tanaka led eight destroyers to the island, he was intercepted by a larger US flotilla and despite enjoying a tactical victory he was forced to retreat and was unable to drop off any supplies for the beleaguered Japanese garrison. It would be the last attempt by the Imperial Navy to supply the island. By December Imperial Naval Command had decided that Guadalcanal would have to be abandoned, a decision ratified by Japanese headquarters on 31 December.

Back on the island, the Japanese forces continued the fight with almost suicidal conviction, but they were gradually pushed further and further north, although this did allow the Imperial Navy to evacuate 10,650 men. By February 1943 Guadalcanal was in American hands.

Casualties on Guadalcanal were heavy. The US Army suffered 6,111 casualties with 1,752 killed. Japanese losses topped 20,000 men as well as 860 aircraft and fifteen warships of various sizes and shapes.

Cologne and Frankfurt Have Some More! The Allied Air Offensive, 1942–44

The view of many senior RAF officials during the 1930s was that large-scale bombing raids had the potential to win a war without the need for costly land battles. It was presumed that by bombing and destroying a country's industrial and manufacturing capacity it would quickly affect that country's material ability to wage war as well as significantly demoralising the public. However, the RAF itself had gone a long way to disproving their own theory with victory in the Battle of Britain. Fighter Command had shown it was actually very difficult for one side to smash their opponent to bits with bombing raids, especially if that opponent had a half-decent fighter unit to defend its skies.

Despite this, the chaps at Bomber Command were itching to give the whole strategic bombing thing a good go. After the retreat from Dunkirk long-range bombing was pretty much the only option open to Churchill if he wanted to launch any kind of offensive operation on Germany. And boy did he need to be seen to get on the front foot. The British public were becoming restless.

The early daylight raids heavily relied upon twin-engine bombers with small bomb loads and even smaller engines that were easy targets for the Luftwaffe fighters tasked with defending the Reich. Not surprisingly these raids were very costly and Bomber Command quickly began racking up significant losses of planes and men. So much so, that they were forced to change strategy and begin bombing at night.

Obviously night bombing brought with it its own difficulties and dangers. To find a specific target in the dead of night, regardless of weather conditions was incredibly difficult – it is estimated that just 3 per cent of bombs dropped during these early night raids landed within five miles of the intended target. Yet despite this, Bomber Command was convinced that Germany needed to be bombed, so too was Churchill, indeed on 14

July 1941 while he was attending a banquet at the County Hall he made it clear what was coming Germany's way:

'We ask no favours of the enemy, we seek from them no compunction. On the contrary, if tonight the people of London were asked to cast their vote as to whether conventions should be entered into to stop the bombing of all cities an overwhelming majority would cry no! We will mete out to the Germans the measure and more than the measure that they have meted out to us. We will have no truce or parley with you, or the grisly gang who work your wicked will. You do your worst and we will do our best.'

But in that summer of 1941 it was the Germans meting it out to the British. Big time. By the end of the year there was no visible reduction in enemy production nor had the morale of the German people hit rock bottom, meanwhile the RAF had lost in the region of 700 aircraft. In the corridors of Westminster the mutterings and whispers regarding the performance of Bomber Command grew louder and more intense. Concurrently, the navy and the army were screaming for bombers to help them out in the Atlantic and in the desert. Bomber Command was looking down the barrel – it needed to deliver results and deliver them fast, otherwise the plug would be pulled on any more large-scale bombing initiatives.

Enter Sir Arthur Harris, newly appointed as Commander-in-Chief of Bomber Command in February 1942. He promised a new dawn for Bomber Command and with new tactics and, more importantly, new bombers, he was determined to make a success of the whole operation.

One of the first things Harris did was to change the targets. He had experience of flying at night and realised that it was much easier to identify targets that were situated near the coast as pilots and navigators can use the coastline as a guide and reference. If the bombers could see the coastline, they could follow it until they reached their target destination. With this in mind he pinpointed the German port towns of Lübeck and Rostock as the new targets for Bomber Command, both situated on the northern coastline of Germany. As such the British bombers had no problems locating their targets and during March and April 1942 both towns were put to the sword.

The era of night area bombing had begun and would continue with success for the next three years. It was indiscriminate, it was controversial and it was very deadly, but in the eyes of Bomber Command, it was badly needed.

Area bombing was targeted against key German industrial cities that were critical to the Nazi war effort. One such place was the city of Cologne, and for Cologne Harris had something a bit special planned. In fact he was planning the biggest, baddest, most destructive night of bombing in the history of night bombing.

A thousand-bomber raid.

Now, mounting a night-bombing raid consisting of 1,000 planes was incredibly ambitious. Not least due to the fact that Harris only had 400 operational bombers in frontline units fit and ready to fly. Training schools and reserve squadrons up and down the country were pillaged for any kind of plane that was capable of flying to Cologne and dropping a bomb or two. The plan was to fly the bombers in a 'stream' formation in which all planes flew at the same speed on the same route to the target, thus overwhelming the local defenses with their sheer weight in numbers. The planes at the pointy end of the stream would drop flares and incendiaries to illuminate the target and start a few fires while the bombers that followed simply dropped their bombs onto the area that was burning. Theoretically this would result in more accurate bombing.

The thousand-bomber raid was pencilled in for 27 May 1942.

Bad weather delayed the raid for a few days but on the evening of 30 May, 1,047 bombers and 113 other craft (there to make a nuisance of themselves and occupy German night fighters) took to the skies all over

England. It was a force two and a half times larger than any other RAF raid in history. Cologne didn't know what was about to hit it.

The raid schedule allowed just ninety minutes for all bombers to pass over the target and release their bombs. It was thought that such an intense period of bombing would overwhelm the Cologne fire services and cause firestorms similar to those seen in London during the height of the Blitz. In the end 868 bombers successfully hit the city, dropping in the region of 1,500 tonnes of explosives between them – two-thirds of these were incendiary bombs.

Two-and-a-half thousand fires were started in the city of Cologne that night.

The damage caused was unprecedented. Twelve thousand non-residential buildings were damaged or destroyed including nine hospitals. Only one military building – an anti-aircraft barracks – was destroyed. On top of this, 13,000 homes were destroyed with another 28,000 damaged. Around 500 people were killed, 5,000 people were injured and over 45,000 people saw their homes go up in smoke.

Despite all of the destruction and damage the industrial capacity of Cologne was not affected. Forty-eight hours later it was the turn of the Ruhr city of Essen to be on the receiving end of a monster raid when 956 bombers attacked. Indeed the industrial heartland of the Ruhr got a pounding from Bomber Command night after night, but despite all of this unwanted attention the Nazi war machine continued to operate.

During these massed bombing raids the Germans took quite a beating, but they were still able to dish it out in equal measure. Exeter, Norwich, Bath, York and Canterbury all had special visits from the Luftwaffe. The Germans were also learning how to improve their own air defence systems. An early-warning radar system set up over the North Sea coast (known as the Kammhuber Line after Lieutenant General Josef Kammhuber) was set up and proved very effective in hitting incoming bomber formations before they got anywhere near the Fatherland. With this system in place, Bomber Command soon found itself on the receiving end of a bit of a mauling, day after day.

Fortunately for Harris, he was no longer fighting a lone battle. The US Eighth Air Force had been in England for a while, steadily readying itself for a go at Göring but they also wanted to have another crack at daylight raids. They had heavily armoured planes and were trained to fly in tight formation – a combination that convinced the US air chiefs that they could do what Bomber Command had failed to do: bomb Germany in broad daylight. Moreover, early raids over France on enemy targets seemed to suggest that they might be able to pull it off.

Daylight bombing over Germany, however, would be a whole new ball game.

Luftwaffe pilots quickly figured out a strategy to break up the massed formation of US bombers. By attacking head on and knocking out the lead aircraft, the rest of the attacking wave invariably scattered. Once the bombers were out of formation they were much easier to pick off. Wunderbar!

Yet the raids continued.

In January 1943 Churchill and Roosevelt met at Casablanca and decided to combine UK and US air forces in a huge attempt to soften up Nazi defences in preparation for a seaborne invasion of Western Europe. Weapons factories, U-boat pens, shipyards, transport links and vital oil plants were among those identified as priority targets for a 24/7 round-the-clock precision bombing campaign designed to reduce the Nazi war machine to rubble. One of the most famous raids in this campaign used revolutionary bouncing bombs in an effort to smash vital dams in the Ruhr valley. It was only partially successful however and cost the lives of some of the best crewmen in the business.

All the while Bomber Command kept plugging away on night raids. With better planes such as the Lancaster coming through in large numbers, along with improved navigation techniques and enhanced target indicators and flares, results steadily improved. Harris was more confident than ever that his night bombers could deal a decisive blow at Nazi industry, and in the summer of 1943 he decided it was time to let loose the full might of his new and improved Bomber Command.

Hamburg was about to get it in spades.

As well as new hardware and better navigation, Harris had another trick up his sleeve for Hamburg. Millions of small aluminium strips were dropped onto the city and played havoc with the German anti-aircraft gun aiming equipment.

The effect of the bombing during the hot summer was as spectacular as it was deadly. A tornado of flame ripped through the city, the local fire brigades had no hope of containing the firestorm – it is estimated that in places the temperature reached 1,000 degrees Celsius. But that wasn't the end of it. The Allies continued a tag-team bombing routine from 24 July until 3 August. Each day the US Air Force smashed the city and when night came so did the Lancasters of Bomber Command. By the end of it more than 33,000 people were dead.

During 1944 the bombing raids were increased in an effort to destroy armament production and also push the Luftwaffe back into Germany and away from the Channel and the Atlantic Wall. Between January and June 1944 the Allies delivered 102 major attacks on German cities with Berlin alone hit by seventeen huge raids. By the spring of 1944 the Luftwaffe was on its knees; it was suffering badly from an acute lack of hardware and fuel. One of the key supply routes of fuel for the Luftwaffe was Ploesti in Rumania, however by June 1944 supplies had been reduced by 80 per cent due to constant air attacks. German synthetic fuel plants were hit just as badly – it was a disastrous time for the Luftwaffe who was forced to function practically on fumes!

When General Dwight D. Eisenhower briefed his men on the eve of D-Day he was able to tell them, with some confidence, that if they saw a plane in the sky it would be friendly. This was largely down to the success of the Allied air offensive.

Tanktastic Kursk, 1943

There can be no doubt about it, 1943 had begun very badly for Germany in the fight against Russia. Defeat at Stalingrad and in the Caucasus, as well as setbacks in an around Leningrad, meant it was necessary for the German Army to put something special together in order to win back the initiative in the East.

Remarkably, Hitler actually allowed strategic withdrawals in many areas of the line – something that his generals in the field had been screaming for for months. Thirty divisions were pulled back approximately 100 miles over a period of three weeks in an effort to straighten up the line that they held. The result was that the line that now needed to be manned had been almost halved to 230 miles.

In the meantime the Russians went on the attack in early 1943, in and around the city of Kharkov. After initial success an overstretched Red Army was eventually driven back by Field Marshal Erich von Manstein's Army Group South, who retook Kharkov and pushed on as far as the city of Belgorod. The result of this action was a large salient (or bulge in the line) that centred on the city of Kursk. Von Manstein was worried that his men would be isolated and proposed to Hitler that his forces dig in and take up strategic defensive positions, wait for the Russians to launch their own offensive and then hit them hard with numerous counterattacks.

It was the sensible strategic option but, not surprisingly, Hitler was having none of it.

An alternative proposal was submitted by von Manstein which saw his men attack Kursk in an effort to pinch off the salient and flatten the line. This new plan pandered much more to Hitler's need to be seen to attack and it was signed off in no time.

On 15 April Hitler issued *Operational Order No. 6*, which called for the Kursk offensive (codenamed Operation *Citadel*) to begin on 3 May or shortly thereafter. The order made it clear that Hitler saw this offensive as an opportunity to show the world that the German war machine was still in fine fettle – many of his commanders saw the offensive slightly differently, thinking that the men and the tanks lost in this battle would have been vital in trying to push back the inevitable Allied invasion in Northern Europe.

Nevertheless, the operational order was issued and the army top brass had little choice in the matter. Operation *Citadel* was going to happen.

Delays hit the planning of the offensive almost immediately. It took a lot longer than estimated to move the required men into position, plus Hitler insisted that the offensive took advantage of a number of new weapons that were just rolling off the Nazi production lines. In his eyes the new tanks (Panthers and Tigers) and the new assault guns (Ferdinands) were essential for victory. In light of this Hitler agreed to put the date of the attack back to 5 July.

The plan for Operation *Citadel* was relatively uncomplicated. There would be two assaults on Kursk – one from the south and one from the north – both of which would be fronted by armoured units packed to the teeth with the hastily produced new hardware. These forces would smash the substantial Red Army presence in the Kursk salient and destroy their reserves, thus severely depleting their ability to launch any future offensives. By doing this, it was presumed that the strategic momentum in the East would swing sharply in favour of the German Army.

On the other side of the wire, the Red Army was also planning its next moves. Stalin was itching to go back on the offensive but Russian intelligence and intense lobbying from his generals convinced him to prepare a strategic defensive operation around Kursk, enticing the Germans to attack a well-organised defensive position which would wear them down, use up vital resources and leave them susceptible to an energetic counterattack. And what a defensive position they put together! The Russian side of the Kursk salient was organised by General

Rokossovsky and General Vatutin, both veterans of Stalingrad. They prepared six separate lines of defenses along with a complex wall of artillery and multiple anti-tank positions. Into these defensive lines they poured over a million men and almost 3,500 tanks – almost forty per cent of the Red Army's total manpower and three-quarters of its armour. This little lot was also backed up by almost 3,000 aircraft. It was a formidable force, and once they were organised, all they had to do was to sit back and wait for the Germans to attack.

Which they duly did on 5 July.

Hitler only decided on that particular date on 1 July but within twenty-four hours Russian intelligence got wind of it and started to prepare accordingly. They still didn't know exactly when the attack would come, but during the night of 4 July a German engineer was caught in No Man's Land and when questioned told his captors that an attack was to be launched at 03:30hrs the following morning.

Cue Russian pre-emptive artillery bombardments.

The might of the Red Army artillery smashed the German lines just as they were getting into position for their own attack, the shells caused panic and mayhem, but the bombardment was not as devastating as Zhukov would have wanted. In most areas up and down the line, the German forces were back in position within an hour. By 04:00hrs the Wehrmacht commanders had made the necessary adjustments and their men were ready to go.

By 05:00hrs, following on the back of a fifty-minute artillery bombardment which saw German guns fire more shells than they had during the entire campaigns in France and Poland combined, the German Ninth Army was attacking in the north and the Fourth Panzer Army was on the move in the south. It was time for the greatest tank battle in history to begin.

The Germans had seventeen panzer divisions in position and ready for a fight. Amongst these were some of the most iconic and fabled divisional names in military history: *Das Reich, Grossdeutschland, SS Totenkopf, Wiking* and *Leibstandarte SS Adolf Hitler.*

In the south, General Hoth's Fourth Panzer Army smashed through what was the weakest part of the Russian defensive line and within forty-eight hours had progressed twenty miles. In the north, however it was a slightly different story, General Model and his Ninth Panzer Army had rolled smack bang into the teeth of some serious Red Army defensive lines. On 6 July Model pushed over 1,000 tanks forward on a front just six miles wide, but the offensive quickly bogged down under murderous Russian fire and had to be called off.

In the south things were still going swimmingly. By 11 July Hoth had managed to get some of his forward formations across the Psel River – the last natural barrier before Kursk and was loudly knocking on the door to Prokhorovka. Lying in wait on the other side of the river was the much-reinforced Russian Fifth Guards Tank Army commanded by General Pavel Rotmistrov.

It was about to get heavy at Prokhorovka.

Early on 12 July, hundreds of Soviet tanks, all carrying infantry, rolled out of Prokhorovka and advanced at high speed in a charge straight at the startled Germans. When machine-gun fire, armor-piercing shells and artillery fire struck the T-34s, the infantry jumped off and sought cover. Leaving these men behind, the T-34s rolled on but most were taken out by the Germans. During a lull in the fighting the Germans took the opportunity to move their big guns into position – it was time for the Tigers.

Another full-scale attack over open ground by the Russian 181st Tank Regiment saw them run straight down the barrel of a large group of SS Tiger tanks. In this kind of fight there was only one winner. The Tiger tank had a monumental 88mm gun and super-thick front armour, rendering it almost unbeatable in long-range combat. The 181st Tank Regiment was annihilated.

Meanwhile, *Das Reich* began their advance from the outskirts of Prokhorovka but was quickly engaged by aggressive pockets of tanks from the II Tank Corps and II Guards Tank Corps, backed up by ground troops and air attacks. The Russians continued to throw more armour at *Das Reich* all day but the Germans went on to push slowly towards Prokhorovka, advancing into the night while suffering relatively light tank losses.

On the left-hand side of the German line *SS Totenkopf* was trying to protect its bridgehead over the River Psel against huge Russian attacks. Once again the Russians threw everything but the kitchen sink at the Germans, but somehow they managed to continue their march on Prokhorov.

Over the next few days the battle raged without either side conjuring up a decisive blow. On 14 July several Soviet rifle divisions were encircled to the south of Prokhorovka and the *Totenkopf* Division took several tactically important hills on the north edge of the town. It seemed that slowly but surely the Panzers were getting their own way.

But then the Allies landed in Sicily and ruined the party in the East. Hitler decided to cancel Operation *Citadel*, despite von Manstein pleading to be allowed to finish off the Russians. Instead of going in for the kill Hitler split his panzers up, pulling a good chunk of them out of Russia to bolster the Italian front. With the momentum lost, the Russians went on the counterattack, retaking Kharkov and even crossing the Dnieper River – often viewed back in Berlin as the German 'Eastern Wall'.

The road was now clear to drive the Germans all the way back to the Fatherland.

Tunisia, Sicily and the Emergence of the Second Front, 1943

When the Nazi Blitzkrieg smashed its way into Russia in June 1941 Winston Churchill was delighted. Russia was in his corner fighting the common enemy of National Socialism. Stalin, however, was slightly less delighted. In the first three weeks of the Russian campaign his Red Army took an absolute pasting at the hands of the Wehrmacht while his new-found friends seemed to just sit back and watch from a safe distance. An icy telegram sent to Churchill on 18 July 1942 was simple and to the point: open up a second front to help the Red Army. Now.

The Allied top brass did not need an angry Russian to tell them about the importance of launching an invasion of mainland Europe, thus opening up a second front. They had been mulling it over since Dunkirk. In October 1941 Winston Churchill told Captain Lord Louis Mountbatten to prepare for the invasion of Europe, explaining that: *'Unless we can go on land and fight Hitler and beat his forces on land, we shall never win this war.'* On the other side of the Channel, the German high command also knew that the fighting would eventually heat up in the West, hence the frantic building of the Atlantic Wall.

The question was not if there would be an invasion but when and where it would take place.

The Americans were itching for a fight and by mid-1942 had already drawn up plans for a full-on invasion of France sometime in 1943. The British hated the idea, thinking it was a suicide mission. Churchill favoured an invasion from North Africa, coming up from the south. As he saw it, southern Europe was the *'soft belly of the crocodile'* and represented the most realistic chance of success. He was convinced an invasion in the south would shorten the war considerably.

The Americans hated that idea even more than the British hated their French plan.

They hated it so much that there were even mutterings about US forces pulling out of Europe altogether to concentrate on giving the Japanese a good kicking in the Pacific. Churchill needed to act fast and in July he somehow persuaded Roosevelt to sign off on his southern plan, although he did commit Britain to a full-scale cross-channel invasion of France as soon as it was realistically possible.

With this mini-crisis averted, Churchill now had the small matter of convincing Stalin that the second front should be Africa and not France. They met in Moscow on 10 August 1942. Stalin was not impressed, but he didn't really have much choice but to accept the Anglo-American decision to invade in the south.

It was all set then. For the Allies in 1943, all roads led to Rome.

Before any excursion to Sicily and Italy could take place, the Allies still had to take care of business in North Africa. Although by the beginning of 1943 Rommel and his Afrika Korps had been pushed right back, they still occupied a decent amount of land in and around Tunisia, including vital ports. They had also enjoyed significant reinforcements during the winter. That said, with the British Eighth Army closing rapidly from the East and the Americans coming in from the West after the success of Operation *Torch*, it was surely just a matter of time before the Germans were kicked out of Africa.

Wasn't it?

Actually no. In a sudden and furious attack along the Kasserine Pass (in Tunisia), Rommel succeeded in socking it to the Americans in one of their most devastating defeats of the entire war. Too experienced, too battle hardened and packing too much power for the smaller American tanks, the Afrika Korps swept them aside. American morale was badly shaken. For the average GI reality well and truly struck in the desert.

Unfortunately for Rommel, he lacked the strength to truly capitalise on his initial breakout. The Americans dusted themselves down, regrouped and within ten days had retaken the pass. For the Germans, evacuation by sea was impossible due to heavy Allied naval presence in the south, and when a forward patrol of the British Eighth Army eventually linked up with the American II Corps, any thought of escape inland was out of the question.

The Afrika Korps was trapped and surrounded. It would only end in tears. After seven days of intense bombardment from the air and from massed artillery, it was all over. The Afrika Korps surrendered. Almost a quarter of a million men were taken prisoner.

It goes without saying that this victory was a major boost for the Allies, especially for Churchill and his southern Europe strategy. Sicily was now the next scheduled stop on the journey and barely two months after the fall of the Afrika Korps, Allied troops led by General Montgomery and General Patton were wading ashore on Sicilian beaches. The Italian defenders were very quick to wave the white flag with many regiments surrendering without a shot being fired. Meanwhile, Allied air attacks on Rome convinced many Italians that the war was up. They turned on their government and kicked Mussolini out of power in July that year. The new government publicly declared that the war would go on, however they immediately started secret negotiations with the Allies for peace.

After just a few weeks almost all of Sicily was in Allied hands with most of the original German occupation force left with no choice but to evacuate to the Italian mainland with Montgomery itching to give chase.

Armistice and Invasion: Italy, 1943

On 3 September 1943 Italy signed terms that set in motion them disengaging from the Axis and joining the Allies. On the very same day Montgomery landed on the mainland encountering no resistance.

It seemed that the whole of Italy was there for the taking.

The Germans had not deserted Italy, but had simply moved north to occupy better defensive positions. The Italians wanted the Allies to point their main invasion fleet way up the coast to protect Rome from German occupation, but the Allies were not keen on that – it was beyond their air cover limits and way too risky. They agreed on a compromise, the town of Salerno – halfway up the coast, right on the limit of range for Allied aircraft.

The invasion force that headed out to Salerno was very limited in its scale, not least because it had been put together at speed in an effort to take advantage of the situation, but also because the Americans insisted that the invasion of France, which was being planned back in the UK, should take priority when it came to resources. Halfway across the waters, the invasion forces heard the news that Italy had formally surrendered and a military armistice was put in place.

Back in Berlin, Hitler was annoyed, but not surprised. He immediately pushed more troops into Italy, quickly passing through Rome and occupying defensive positions in and around Salerno. When the Allied troops landed, they would be ready with the welcome party.

The Allied landing forces were met with ferocious firepower, after forty-eight hours the beachhead was so precarious that American generals seriously considered getting the hell out of there and re-embarking, but with huge support from air and sea the invaders just about managed to hold on and after a week of savage hand-to-hand fighting, the Germans eventually withdrew. They moved up the country to the mountains south of Rome, here, encouraged by their near victory at Salerno, they received reinforcements, dug in and waited.

Meanwhile, for the Allies after this very sticky start things started to ease off slightly – within three weeks they had captured the important port city of Naples. Most of southern Italy was in Allied hands – the whole situation was looking much more rosy. As they marched north, they hoped that Hitler had perhaps ordered a full retreat of the Wehrmacht.

Alas, no.

The man in charge of the German forces in Italy was Field Marshal Kesselring. As far as defensive terrain goes, the natural landscape offered up by Italy was almost perfect. A large line of mountains runs through the length of Italy almost like a backbone. These mountains are practically impossible for infantry to pass, which forced the Allies to take the narrow coast roads either side. The only hope for the Allies of outflanking the Germans would be to take to the sea, but the necessary landing craft and supplies needed for such a venture had been pinched by the chaps organising D-Day.

This was going to be one tough advance.

It was made even tougher by the retreating Germans trashing rail networks, blowing bridges and destroying roads and telephone systems as they went. Any towns they passed through were systematically riddled with deadly booby-traps. By winter, the Eighth Army, accustomed to dashing across North African sand at breakneck speed, was up to its knees in Italian mud and had been reduced to tiny daily advances measured in metres, not miles. The Americans were not faring much better.

Italy was proving to be far from the 'soft underbelly' that Churchill had first envisioned. Indeed, it was more like a tough old gut.

It wasn't until the winter of 1943 that the Allies began to knock on the door of Kesselring's defensive line. He had nine full divisions, with another eight hiding in the shadows, ready to be called upon if needed. The Americans, attempting to go over the mountains, had eleven. It was a slow, costly slog. Every house on every street of every tiny Italian mountain town and village had to be fought over. It would often take days, even weeks, just to clear one village before going on to the next one.

The Allied advance was quickly grinding to a halt.

At the Tehran conference in November 1943 Churchill was told in no uncertain terms by Roosevelt and Stalin that from now on the priority for the Allies would be the preparation of a full-on invasion of France, which at that time was pencilled in for May 1944. As a result, Italy was reduced to a sideshow. Undeterred, Churchill lobbied hard and managed to get the nod for one last go at Hitler's Italian defenses.

Somehow he managed to beg, borrow and steal enough landing craft together for a new amphibious attack on the Italian coast. Once more, it was game on in Italy.

Anzio and Cassino, 1944

Churchill's new plan was made up of two separate phases: first the American Fifth Army would attack the Germans at Cassino, breaching the Gustav Line – a string of fortified defensive positions that crossed Italy south of Rome. This, it was hoped, would draw forces based in and around Rome south to help out with the fight, using up vital German reserves. Then an amphibious attack would strike behind the German lines at Anzio, just twenty-two miles south of Rome. It was expected that the shock of this Allied one-two would provoke the Germans into giving up the Gustav Line and falling back north of Rome.

The area of the Gustav Line chosen to be attacked was dominated by the imposing Monte Cassino, a rocky hill rising up over 500 metres which is crowned by an ancient Benedictine monastery. The US Fifth Army attacked Cassino on 20 January 1944. The men trying to capture the German defensive positions – all situated on high ground with a commanding view – had already fought their way through southern Italy, including some very tough mountain terrain. They had not been reinforced and were exhausted before they even started this new attack at Cassino.

Not surprisingly it was an utter disaster.

Churchill was not going to stop though, no way, and forty-eight hours later the seaborne attack on Anzio commenced. Even though the Germans had an inkling that some kind of coastal attack was coming, they didn't know where and they simply didn't have enough men and resources to defend all of Italy's coast. As such, the Allies waded ashore at Anzio completely unopposed and had a beachhead in place without a shot being fired, a few of the senior officers could have been forgiven if they started to wonder if perhaps this was the opportunity for them to dish out some Blitzkrieg of their own and smash their way through to Rome in the blink of an eye.

Or perhaps not. The man in charge on the ground – a certain General Lucas – was a cautious chap who was a firm believer that slow and steady wins the race. He was not prepared to march one inch inland until the beachhead was fully secured. Churchill was incandescent at this lack of activity, likening Lucas to a whale floundering on the beach. Hindsight is a wonderful thing of course, but due to the fact that Field Marshal Kesselring was at that time organising his army for a very swift and very violent counterattack – it is very probable that the scratch force that Lucas had brought ashore would have been torn to pieces had they gone on the attack.

As it was, they got a mauling from Kesselring anyway. Allied advance units sent out by Lucas to form a defensive perimeter around the beachhead were almost completely destroyed, leaving Lucas's troops at the mercy of their enemy. The only way to get help to Lucas was to bring in reinforcements from the exact place he was meant to be helping break – the Gustav Line, more specifically, Monte Cassino.

The first attack at Monte Cassino had cost in the region of 14,000 Allied casualties. A second attack was planned for early February 1944, but General Freyberg, commanding the New Zealand men that were going to be part of the new assault, insisted that the monastery be bombed just in case the Nazis were using it as a fortress.

On 15 February over 200 heavy and medium bombers combined to blow the monastery to bits. Ironically it was only when the bombers had finished their work that the Germans actually moved in to occupy the monastery, the ruins of which provided excellent defensive positions.

That same day Freyberg sent his New Zealanders off to capture the Cassino railway station whilst the 4th Indian Division attacked what was left of the monastery. After just a matter of days the offensive was called off after achieving next to nothing. General Alexander, the Allied Commander in Italy, wanted to wait until the spring before having another go at Monte Cassino, but, under immense pressure from London and Washington to relieve the Anzio beachhead he reluctantly agreed to launch a third assault.

On 15 March more bombers were thrown into the mix, smashing the town of Cassino as well as the surrounding area in an attempt to soften up the German defenses. Once the dust had settled the New Zealand Corps once more tried to storm the town, but after taking over 4,000 casualties in just one week the attack was called off.

Monte Cassino was proving a formidable obstacle.

In May 1944 Alexander launched what would be the final assault. Operation *Diadem* was a large operation incorporating French, British, Polish, New Zealand, South African and American forces. The initial plan was to move the majority of the British Eighth Army from the Adriatic front across the spine of Italy to join the US Fifth Army and attack along a twenty-mile front between Cassino and the sea. With the arrival of the spring weather it was hoped that ground conditions would be good enough to deploy large formations of men and armour effectively.

At 23:00hrs on 11 May the attack kicked off with a massive artillery bombardment made up of 1,600 guns. Within ninety minutes the thick end of twenty-one fully spec'd infantry divisions were in full advance along the entire front. At first the US II Corps struggled to make any progress, but elsewhere on the front initial momentum was strong. The French quickly gained their objectives, capturing vital areas around Monte Cassino. The French, commanded by General Juin, used men from the Moroccan 4th Mountain Division and Goumiers, a special force of North African mountain dwellers who found little difficulty in conquering the very difficult terrain. They effectively cut off the German forces, who were concentrating their efforts at Monte Cassino, and opened up a clear route to Rome. Meanwhile, Indian engineers had succeeded in building a bridge across the River Rapido (which ran directly in front of the Gustav Line) which enabled the 1st Canadian Armoured Brigade to get into the teeth of the battle – something the Allies were unable to do in their first two attempts at taking the position.

By 15 May the British managed to isolate the town of Cassino, two days later the Polish II Corps launched their attack on the monastery. Under constant artillery and mortar fire from the strongly fortified German positions and with little natural cover for protection, the fighting was brutal and they lost 3,500 men but they eventually occupied the monastery on 18 May, only to find it empty apart from a handful of wounded Germans. The rest had fled. Kesselring ordered the retreat north to the so-called Gothic Line, north of Florence.

Finally – after five months, four separate offensives and 55,000 casualties – the route from the south was open and the road to Rome was clear.

Operation *Longcloth*: The Chindits in Burma, 1943–44

After being unceremoniously kicked out of Burma in April 1942 the British Indian forces needed some time to take stock of the situation and lick their wounds. On the other side of the fence the Japanese had stretched themselves as far as they could and the state of their supply lines dictated that they were not able to go on any further.

Stalemate ensued.

Back in India, the Allied commander-in-chief of the region, General Archibald Wavell, started to hatch a plan that would enable him to recapture central Burma and re-open the vital supply line known as the Burma Road. In planning this new attack Wavell called in one of the most unorthodox officers of the British Army – Major General Orde Wingate – who had served under Wavell in Palestine in the 1930s and also commanded a guerilla unit which fought in East Africa in 1940–41. Wingate was sometimes rude, always opinionated and ever so slightly eccentric, but he had often touted the idea of long-range penetration groups, made up of insanely fit men highly trained in the art of guerilla warfare, as the perfect way to weaken the Japanese grip on Burma.

Wingate was convinced the only way to win was to fight in the jungle, away from the roads and rivers which would almost always be heavily defended. His men would be dropped behind enemy lines from the air and they would also be supplied from the air, so they didn't have to carry lots of equipment. Once on the ground they would be able to quickly infiltrate enemy strongpoints, cut communication lines, destroy bridges and generally cause a nuisance.

Wavell was eventually persuaded to allow a small experimental operation to go ahead. Operation *Longcloth* was provisionally scheduled for February 1943. His men, known as Chindits, were about to get their chance.

About 3,000 men took part in Operation *Longcloth* – the majority were dropped from gliders into the jungle on the night of 14/15 February 1943. During the next four weeks the Chindits penetrated more than 500 miles into enemy territory. They blew up railway lines, destroyed bridges and fought at least nine engagements with Japanese forces. After four weeks, they had reached the limits of their air supply lines; they had lost over 800 men, they were exhausted, dangerously short of rations and riddled with disease, but they had proven Wingate's theory to be true. In one last defiant act before they returned to base they set up an ambush for the Japanese in which a hundred enemy soldiers were killed for the loss of just one single Chindit.

Operation *Longcloth* was deemed a success, so much so that Wingate was given access to mountains of equipment and resources and told to plan a second, much more extensive raid.

On 5 March 1944 British, Indian and Ghurka men were once more dropped by glider behind enemy lines into the Burmese jungle. The Americans wanted to open a supply route to China from India and this required the capturing of Japanese-held north Burma. To achieve this an American-led Chinese force commanded by US Army General Alexander Stilwell advanced from the north into Burma. By April there were over 9,000 officers and men marauding behind Japanese lines.

The Chindits' objective was to cut the supply lines of the Japanese forces facing British, American and Chinese forces in north Burma. The key priority was to cut the communication lines to the forces facing Stilwell's advance. However, on 24 March 1944, Wingate, by then a Major-General, was killed in a plane crash. Wingate's death was a serious blow to the Chindits and changed the course of the rest of the campaign. In an attempt to keep up morale, Admiral Lord Mountbatten, Commander-in-Chief South East Asia Command, issued the following *Order of the Day to Special Forces*:

'General Wingate has been killed in the hour of his triumph. The Allies have lost one of the most forceful and dynamic personalities that this war has produced. You have lost the finest and most inspiring leader a force could have wished for, and I have lost a personal friend and faithful supporter. He has lit the torch. Together we must grasp it and carry it forward. Out of your gallant and hazardous expedition into the heart of Japanese-held territory will grow the final reconquest of Burma and the ultimate defeat of the Japanese. He was so proud of you. I know you will live up to his expectations.'

After Wingate's death, the Chindits were put under the direct control of General Stilwell and were forced to take up a role of normal infantry. It was a role they were neither equipped nor trained to do. Not surprisingly they took heavy casualties in the ensuing battles – in fact it is estimated that 90 per cent of all Chindit casualties in their second operation occurred under the command of the US Army.

After a particularly vicious fight for a hill codenamed Point 2171 which lasted two weeks, Mountbatten ordered that the Chindits be withdrawn from the frontline for some well-earned rest and to be inspected by doctors. Exhaustion and illness were taking a huge toll on the men and when the doctors inspected them they found only a hundred of them were fit enough to continue the fight. When the medical reports were received, Mountbatten ordered Stilwell to evacuate the sick and wounded immediately and it was agreed that the remaining Chindit brigades would be withdrawn.

The last Chindits left Burma on 27 August 1944. This second campaign had cost them 3,628 casualties.

Bleeding to Death in the East: Winter, 1943

After missing a massive opportunity at Kursk, the Wehrmacht were put to the sword by the Red Army. Stalin immediately ordered a counterattack along the whole of the Soviet–German front – he smelt blood. Nazi blood. And he wanted to spill as much of it as humanly possible. Stalin's plan was simple: push the Axis forces back across the Dnepr River and isolate them in the Crimea and kick them out of the Moscow area for good.

As the German armies fled they destroyed everything in their path, leaving the local population without food, shelter or dignity. In the south, von Manstein's Army Group South consisted of forty-two divisions, still a sizeable force, but they were being hunted by a massive force of 120 divisions that was constantly being reinforced and strengthened. By early August the Russians had succeeded in driving a huge wedge into von Manstein's army, allowing them to liberate Belgorod, Bogodukhov and eventually the city of Kharkov, which fell on 22 August.

Hitler was so worried by the news reports from the front that he travelled out to see what was going on for himself, spending a week with von Manstein in early September. Eventually he agreed to allow his men to pull back all the way to the Dnepr River and by 21 September almost 750,000 German troops had reached and crossed the Dnepr. It was hoped that here they would be able to dig in, reorganise and form some kind of defensive position to fend off the Red Army.

They were to be disappointed.

By 25 September the Russians had established forty bridgeheads on either side of the river, not surprisingly most of these bridgeheads saw brutal fighting over the next few weeks. Most, but not all. There was one small bridgehead, located in swampy land around the village of Liutezh, which the Germans didn't worry too much about. There was no way any army could get across the marsh. Could they?

The Red Army thought they could. In fact they chose that area as the jumping-off point for an all-out assault on Kiev and during late October the entire Russian 3rd Guards Tank Corps was moved into the marshland completely undetected. On 3 November they attacked.

Von Manstein had expected an attack at some point, but he had expected it to come from the dry bridgeheads from the south – not the swampy lands in the north. Thirty Russian infantry divisions, backed by 1,500 tanks made easy work of the German defenders. The city of Kiev was back in Russian hands within three days and after a fierce German counterattack ultimately failed to push the Red Army back, the city was secured on 7 November. Back in Moscow, news of the recapture of Kiev was celebrated with a magnificent fireworks display.

The Russians were not content with their gains though. They wanted to kick the Germans out of Russia for good and continued their push eastwards. By the end of December 1943 a depleted German Army was in full retreat all along the Eastern Front. The Red Army had managed to advance over a hundred miles beyond Kiev and had cleared Axis troops from two-thirds of the territory they had occupied at the limit of their advance. Yet Stalin urged his men forward still, he had his eyes on a very specific prize.

Berlin.

Wolkenkuckucksheim: The Atlantic Wall, 1941–43

Berlin, 11 December 1941. Adolf Hitler addresses the Reichstag with an eighty-eight minute monologue in which he announces to the world that Germany is now at war with the United States of America.

Not content with that small bombshell, the Führer also mentioned for the first time his vision of making Europe an *'impregnable fortress'*. He went on to boast with much gusto that *'...from Kirkenes* [on the Norwegian/Finnish border] *to the Spanish frontier stretches the most extensive belt of great defence installations and fortresses... I am determined to make this European front impregnable against any enemy attack.'*

It was a bold claim; the length of territory mentioned in this speech was the thick end of 3,000 miles – that's a lot of fortifications. The line wasn't as extensive as he liked to make out either. Indeed, at the time of his speech, the Pas de Calais area of France – the area of coastline where most German staff officers expected an Allied invasion to occur – had precisely zero fortifications in place.

There was a lot of work to do if Hitler's dream of a fortified Europe was to become a reality, but Hitler was nothing but persistent, and he demanded that his generals build him the biggest, baddest defence system the world had ever seen. On 23 March 1942 Hitler issued *Führer Directive No. 40* which, in anticipation of a large-scale Allied invasion, stipulated that the Atlantic coastal defences should be designed in such a way so that any invasion attempt would be smashed to pieces either before the main landing force had a chance to reach land or immediately afterwards. He wanted 15,000 concrete strongpoints manned by 300,000 soldiers, and as no one really knew where the invasion would occur, the whole of the coastline had to be defended. And by the way, the entire defence system needed to complete by 1 May 1943.

The man in charge of making the Atlantic Wall a reality was Field Marshal Karl Gerd von Rundstedt, a career soldier who came out of retirement in 1939 and, after masterminding the successful flanking of the Maginot Line in 1940 that ultimately led to the collapse of France, was given the role of Supreme Commander West. This role ultimately put von Rundstedt in control of all of the occupied Western territories.

Thousands upon thousands of slave labourers, staff from the German state construction group (Organisation Todt) and civilian workers from the local population were forced to work twenty-four hours a day building the concrete fortifications, gun emplacements, pillboxes and assorted other structures that made up the wall. Eye-watering amounts of concrete, steel girders and other raw materials were used up in the process. There were such chronic shortages of raw materials that parts of the French Maginot Line and the German Siegfried Line (both massive defensive lines made up of hundreds of forts and strongpoints running hundreds of miles along the French/German border) were dismantled and used to bolster the Atlantic Wall. The original deadline of 1 May 1943 came and went – it had always been an unrealistic target.

Towards the end of 1943 around half a million men were busy building Hitler's defence system. It was starting to take shape, but progress was still too slow. In the autumn, Field Marshal von Rundstedt asked Hitler for more resources to help finish the job. In response to this request Hitler sent Rommel.

On his return from Africa, Field Marshal Erwin Rommel had been given command of Army Group B, and with that came responsibility for the coastal defences of northern France. Rommel was also given an explicit directive to evaluate and inspect the coastal defences of the rest of the Atlantic Wall and report back directly to the Führer's headquarters with his findings. Seeing this as a move that undermined his authority in the region, von Rundstedt was less than impressed.

Rommel was not exactly jumping for joy with what he saw on his initial inspection either. He had spent the last few years fighting in Africa and hadn't set a foot in France since 1941. He had heard all about the Atlantic Wall and, like most of the German population, he was under the impression that it was a spectacular defence system that was pretty much completed and ready to knock any British and American invasion straight back into the sea. He was to be disappointed.

In Rommel's opinion, the Atlantic Wall was farcical; he even went as far as calling it a 'figment of Hitler's *Wolkenkuckucksheim* (cloud cuckoo land).'

Rommel was convinced that the invasion battle, and indeed the entire war, would be won and lost on the beaches. He knew that the best chance the German Army had of repelling any large-scale invasion would be when the enemy was still in the sea, before they got any kind of foothold on land. He was known to say on many occasions that: *'The first twenty-four hours of the invasion will be decisive...'* With the backing of both Hitler and von Rundstedt, Field Marshal Rommel set about building a defensive structure that might have a chance of stopping any invasion force in their tracks.

It was time to get busy.

On every beach that could feasibly handle an invasion force, huge numbers of anti-invasion obstacles were erected. These were an assortment of jagged sections of steel girders, concrete bollards and metal-tipped wooden stakes, many of which were adorned with anti-tank Teller mines or artillery shells that were primed to explode on just the slightest impact. These were placed just below high and low tide water marks and were specifically designed to rip apart troop-filled landing craft or at least delay them long enough to enable shore-based guns to zero in on their targets.

In and around the beaches, especially the pathways that led off inland, Rommel had his men sow immense minefields designed to stop the Allied force penetrating too far too fast. By the summer of 1944 approximately 5 million mines of various designs had been planted.

Behind these vast belts of anti-tank and anti-personnel mines Rommel's men took up their positions in the concrete bunkers, gun emplacements and pillboxes. They were all linked together using underground tunnels and included offices, latrines, kitchens, water and ventilation systems and first aid posts. Thick belts of barbed wire and yet more minefields encircled these strongpoints in such a way as to funnel any attacking force into killing zones covered by machine-gun nests with interlocking fields of fire.

Every available artillery gun at Rommel's disposal was trained on the beaches and the sea. To supplement this firepower Rommel also used a few different offensive techniques, including rocket launchers, miniature robot tanks that could carry more than half a tonne of explosives via a remote control device, plus huge flamethrowers *(Abwehrflammenwerfer)* that could produce a sheet of flame almost three metres high and four metres wide. The flame was delivered via the touch of a button through pipes that were dug into sand dunes, making these weapons particularly nasty.

Further inland, great tracts of land were purposefully flooded to hinder enemy paratroopers. Any area within seven or eight miles of the coast that could be used as landing grounds for gliders was covered with large heavy wooden stakes nicknamed *Rommelspargeln* (Rommel's Asparagus). These stakes were booby-trapped with explosives and trip wires.

Field Marshal Rommel had organised the most hostile welcoming party ever seen. There was nothing left for him to do but wait for the inevitable. He knew the Allies were coming. He just didn't quite know where or when.

D-Day: 6 June 1944

The Allies had been scratching their heads trying to figure out the logistics of launching an amphibious invasion against western France for a number of years. The US Army (more specifically Army Chief-of-Staff General George C. Marshall) was itching for a fight with Germany and was pushing for an invasion of France from as early as mid-1942. At that time it was dismissed out of hand by Churchill – Britain was just not ready. Yet.

The thought of a French invasion never went away though and in early 1943 General Sir Frederick Morgan was appointed to the post of Chief of Staff to the Supreme Allied Commander (this title was soon shortened to COSSAC) and was given a brief to begin preparations for *'...a full-scale assault against the continent in 1944 as early as possible.'*

The chaps at COSSAC had a choice of two landing zones – Calais or Normandy – and over the course of 1943 they developed a plan that would see an invasion force assault France on a narrow front in Normandy. Although Normandy was much further away from Calais, it had two redeeming features that made it the landing zone of choice: firstly it was not as strongly fortified and defended (the Nazis were convinced that the Allies would be knocking on the door at Calais, so concentrated much of their defence efforts in that part of France); and secondly, the beaches in Normandy were not all surrounded by cliffs and offered multiple exit points, making them much more suited to the landing of an invasion force – on paper at least.

The plans put forward by COSSAC were rubber stamped by Churchill and Roosevelt during meetings at Quebec in August 1943. The invasion would take place in May 1944 and would be given a brand new codename: *Overlord*.

On 7 December 1943 General Eisenhower met with President Roosevelt in Tunis where he was informed he would be commanding the invasion. Later that month a secret mission was undertaken to collect sand from the beaches of Normandy. The sand was analysed and tested; the results were good. It was deemed that the beaches would be able to handle the heavy traffic of an invasion force.

Overlord was on.

In January 1944 Eisenhower established SHAEF (Supreme Headquarters Allied Expeditionary Forces) at Bushey Park on the outskirts of London and quickly gathered around him some of the brightest minds in the Allied ranks, including General Bernard Montgomery who was appointed as the Commander-in-Chief in the field. Once all the seats on the SHAEF top table had been filled, Eisenhower got busy orchestrating what would become the largest seaborne invasion in history.

The original invasion plan, devised by COSSAC in 1943, called for landings by three infantry divisions and two airborne divisions in Normandy. The naval requirements for such an undertaking were significant: over 3,300 landing craft of all shapes and sizes, over 450 warships of various designs, along with 150 minesweepers to clear a path to the beaches.

However, when SHAEF and Eisenhower got in on the planning act the first thing they did was widen out the invasion front so that Cherbourg was reachable and the German reinforcements were stretched over a wider area. This larger front needed more men, more rations, more equipment and more landing craft. The scale of the invasion was enormous. 75,000 British and Canadian men along with 57,500 American, 900 armoured vehicles and 600 big guns needed a massive armada of ships to get them ashore. Over 7,000 vessels were required with about 200,000 sailors working on them. The assault fleet itself would see over 1,200 ships including 300 warships and over 4,000 landing craft. If this little lot was not enough, the seaborne assault would be backed up by almost 12,000 aircraft.

In the run up to invasion both British and American manufacturing industries were pushed to breaking point.

To keep an army of this size moving once in France required more fuel than could be supplied via the sea – they needed another way. Allied scientists came up with a brilliant solution: PLUTO (Pipe Line Under The Ocean) was a revolutionary cross-channel pipeline that ran from the Isle of Wight to the Cherbourg Peninsular. Construction started in August 1944 and was finished in a matter of weeks. By VE Day it had delivered 170 million gallons of fuel to the invasion army. It was an incredible feat of engineering.

If the liberation of Europe was to be successful, the Allies would need more than fuel. They would need to be able to reinforce the initial landings with hundreds of thousands more men and vehicles, along with all the rations, ammunition and supplies essential to keep the army advancing in good order. The only major port in the vicinity of the invasion beaches was Cherbourg and the Allies knew they couldn't guarantee this port would be of any use to them; they had to come up with a different solution. The answer was quite literally towed across the English Channel with the invasion fleet – two prefabricated concrete 'Mulberry' harbours, each the size of Dover, that were sunk into position to form a makeshift port. The first one was up and running by 14 June and, despite one being destroyed in a storm, the remaining Mulberry continued to be used and in one hundred days 2,500,000 men, 500,000 vehicles and 4,000,000 tonnes of equipment and rations were unloaded from its floating roadways.

During the spring of 1944, Eisenhower met regularly with his commanders to ensure everything was going to plan. One topic that was always high on the agenda was that of deception. If the invasion was to be a success the Nazis must have absolutely no idea what was going on. To keep the Germans guessing, the Allies put together plans for a number of fake invasions that they knew would get into Nazi hands. One of the more elaborate hoaxes was that of using Scotland as the base for an invasion of Denmark but the Allies spent a lot of time and effort trying to convince Hitler that they were indeed going to make their main assault in the Pas de Calais region. The Allies called this deception *Fortitude South*. A huge ghost army – the First US Army Group – was 'created' and groups of 'real-life' radio operators spent weeks sending out false radio messages that often made references to invasion-related topics. Thousands of dummy planes, tanks, guns, jeeps and other equipment were manufactured to fool Nazi reconnaissance planes and a huge but completely fake oil dock was built at Dover.

The Nazis were quickly fooled. It was quite beautiful.

Meanwhile, throughout the spring of 1944 the RAF and USAAF were doing their best to smash as much of German-occupied France to smithereens with concentrated bombing raids on communication hubs and transportation links. At the same time, the south of England was rapidly being transformed into one vast army camp as the build-up of troops and equipment needed for the invasion began to be brought together in readiness. By May 1944 there was the thick end of 3 million troops under arms in southern England, all waiting for the nod to get going and give the Germans a good hiding.

On 8 May General Eisenhower formally set the final date for Overlord. It would be Y plus 4. Y-Day was 1 June, this was the date when all preparations were to be completed and the army, navy and air force would be all ready to go. Therefore *Overlord* was set for 5 June 1944.

The last few days of May were hot. Very hot. And the hot weather did nothing to help the nerves and the tension of the men as they boarded ships and waited for the order to get going. On 1 June some of the more distant convoys located in the north of England and Wales started on their journey to their ultimate jumping-off points. The first tentative moves of the invasion were underway.

Despite a hot May, the weather during those first days in June quickly turned nasty. By 4 June the weather had deteriorated so much that Field Marshal Rommel left France to visit his family, convinced that not even the British would be mad enough to launch the biggest invasion in history in gale force winds and torrential rain. He was right, to a point. Back at SHAEF Eisenhower was meeting with his weather advisors twice a day in an effort to figure out whether the invasion would go ahead as planned. The final weather conference was scheduled for 04:00hrs on the morning of 4 June. Convoys were forming up in open seas and final preparations were being made. The weather forecast for 5 June was bad. Very bad. At 06:00hrs on the morning of 4 June he decided to put everything on hold for twenty-four hours.

In the evening of 4 June the meteorologists offered up a glimmer of hope. They anticipated a break in the storm – a window of thirty-six hours of relatively clear weather with only light winds. What's more, Allied bombers, fighters and spotters would be able to operate on the Monday night 5/6 June, although there would be scattered cloud. Eisenhower canvassed opinion from the rest of SHAEF – they were split as to whether to go. It was down to the Supreme Commander. He paced the meeting room in silence, all eyes following him. At 21:45hrs he gave his decision: *'I am quite positive that the order must be given.'*

By 23:00hrs every vessel involved in the invasion had been given the order to resume operations.

D-Day would be 6 June 1944.

Five separate beaches had been identified as landing zones for the invasion. The American First Army, under Lieutenant Omar Bradley, was to attack two beaches on the right flank of the invasion codenamed 'Utah' and 'Omaha'; the British and Canadian forces, under Lieutenant General Miles Dempsey, were to attack 'Gold', 'Juno' and 'Sword' beaches.

As the invasion fleet massed in the Channel during the night of 5 June 1944, six gliders full of men from the Ox and Bucks Light Infantry crossed into France and landed a few miles inland where they quickly secured vital bridges and strategic positions prior to the main amphibious attack. This small band of men were part of a 20,000-strong group of US and British airborne troops that were dropped into France on D-Day with the express objectives of securing both the east (British) and west (American) flanks of the invasion beaches before the main assault could take place. However, due to strong winds many of these paras were blown off course and very few of them were able to carry out their orders effectively. Only one regiment from the US 82nd Airborne Division achieved success when they managed to liberate the village of Sainte-Mère-Église – the first French village to be wrestled from the hands of the Nazis.

As dawn broke on 6 June the invasion force emerged from the sea mist to the complete disbelief of the German defenders. Many were still convinced that any major landing would take place in the Pas de Calais region and as a result, they did not exactly rush to man their guns. Then, in an instant the peaceful still of that summer morning was shattered as the invasion force let rip a monumental naval barrage on to the German coastal defenses, closely followed by massed bomber raids. It was 05.50hrs.

As the naval bombardment of rockets and shells pounded the coastline, thousands of men clambered down dodgy rope ladders from their troop carriers into hundreds of tiny landing craft. The sea was rough and the landing craft were being thrown all over the place by the waves and swell of the water. After the months of training, preparation and waiting the men were finally on their way.

In some sectors the bombardment worked a treat. On Utah Beach, the most westerly of the invasion beaches, the Americans quickly overcame some initial resistance and managed to get 20,000 men and 1,700 vehicles ashore in fifteen hours with just 300 casualties. On Gold Beach the British 50th Infantry Division took heavy casualties in the first wave of men trying to get ashore but eventually managed to land 25,000 men on the beach with just 400 casualties. The Canadian 3rd Division within a matter of hours secured Juno Beach and on Sword Beach the British were just as rapid – liberating the port town of Ouistreham by midday.

On Omaha Beach however, things were a little different.

The beach at Omaha was long and flat, but surrounded by cliffs which offered German guns an eagle-eyed view of the sand. The beach was very heavily fortified and the air strike that was intended to eliminate these defensive positions had failed dismally. So, when the first wave of American troops approached the beach the Germans were waiting for them. The first landing craft hit the beach at 06.31hrs. As they approached it was eerily quiet, some of the men could actually see the German defenders up in the cliffs looking down on them, but they were not firing. It was all a bit weird.

Then the ramps to the landing craft were lowered and all hell was let loose.

In an instant, Omaha Beach was transformed into a blazing inferno. Elite members of the German 352nd Infantry Division defended the beach and their machine-gun fire cut the Americans to pieces as they attempted to leave their landing craft. 'A' Company of 116th US Infantry lost 96 per cent of its effective fighting force before any of them had chance to fire a single round. After just ten minutes 'A' Company had just one officer left breathing. It was the same story up and down the beach – men were being slaughtered on the sand everywhere you looked. By 08:30hrs the situation was so bad that General Bradley seriously considered pulling his men off the beach altogether. In a last ditch effort, a number of naval destroyers were moved up as close to land as possible and ordered to smash seven bells out of the cliffs at what was effectively point blank range. Slowly but surely the German defensive positions in the cliffs were destroyed and by 11:00hrs the tide was turning. By the end of the day 34,000 men were ashore at Omaha and some had managed to push inland up to a mile. Casualties were 2,400.

It had taken almost four years for the Nazis to build the Atlantic Wall. It had taken the Allies less than twenty-four hours to breach it. By midnight on D-Day 130,000 troops had been safely deposited ashore with footholds gained on all five beaches and another 22,000 men dropped in from the sky. Casualties were around 10,000 with 2,500 dead.

Now, it was time to breakout from the beachheads and begin on the tough road to Paris and the true liberation of France.

Bocage: Breakout from Normandy, 1944

Rommel was convinced that the battle would be won and lost on the beaches and had said so publicly on a number of occasions. Field Marshal von Rundstedt, on the other hand, preferred swift and powerful counterattacks using his panzers to push any invasion back into the sea. Hitler was unable to make a proper decision either way and eventually a messy compromise was agreed upon which, in the end, helped no one in the German camp.

The bottom line is that during those first vital hours of the invasion, the officer class of the German Army failed to do their job. They failed to take the initiative, failed to think on their feet in the heat of battle, failed to go with their instinct and failed to trust their training. Ultimately they failed to lead their men. Instead of taking the situation by the scruff of the neck they waited. They waited for orders from headquarters. Orders given to them by some desk-bound staff officer who had no idea what was going on at the beaches. The panzer commanders knew where their enemy was, they knew they were stronger, faster, harder than they were at that moment, they knew that if they acted fast they had a good chance of crushing the invasion before it gained momentum. But they couldn't move. They couldn't move because they didn't have the authority to give orders to their own men. Yes, you read that correctly, the panzer commanders didn't have the authority to give orders to their own men.

Madness.

When it came to the panzers, only Hitler could press the go button and he was asleep. And no one wakes the Führer. Ever. So those panzers just stood still and waited, watching as the window of opportunity slammed shut right in their face.

Within days of the landing, the Allies found themselves up against a stubborn and organised enemy that had recovered well and was starting to fight back strongly. By 10 June only three out of the seven panzer divisions were in the fight trying to throw the Allies back in the sea – the rest were still held back. The Luftwaffe was nowhere to be seen either, the RAF and USAAF had complete air superiority. Domination of the air was utterly vital for the Allies as the two Mulberry harbours delivered thousands of men, vehicles, guns and rations daily. A couple of well-placed Nazi bombs would have ruined the supply of the invading army. As it was the reinforcements kept flooding into France. By 11 June there were 326,000 men and 54,000 vehicles ashore. By the middle of the month over half a million men were lining up to kick the Nazis out of France.

But it was proving tougher than first expected.

The thick hedgerows that crisscrossed the Normandy countryside were a nightmare for Allied tanks and armour, but perfect for setting up tough defensive positions. Snipers had a field day. Progress was slow – almost inch by inch.

By 12 June the five beachheads had finally been linked, providing a combined toe hold on the peninsular that was some sixty miles wide and twenty-five miles deep.

The Allies didn't want to have to rely on the Mulberry harbours as their sole source of reinforcements and had pinpointed the port of Cherbourg as being a prime objective for the invading army to capture as quickly as possible. By 19 June the Americans had cut off the Cherbourg peninsular and were advancing quickly on the town itself. After a fierce battle the German garrison, along with some 25,000 men, surrendered on 26 June. As well as taking the heat off of the Mulberry harbours, the capture of Cherbourg allowed PLUTO (Pipe Line Under The Ocean) to deliver millions of gallons of fuel every day to the Allied armies.

Next on the Allies' hit list was the city of Caen.

Montgomery wanted to take Caen quickly after landing on the beaches. He thought that such an attack would attract the bulk of the German armour, allowing Bradley and his US First Army to break out to the west and sneak around the back of the Germans. However Rommel wasn't having any of it and threw Monty back. Caen remained in German hands and Eisenhower started to get frustrated with the lack of progress on the eastern part of the invasion.

On 18 July Montgomery had another go at Caen. First off, he sent the bombers in – over 2,000 of them to be precise – to smash the town to pieces with high explosive and fragmentation bombs. It was the heaviest bombing raid the Allies had ever put together in support of a ground offensive and was closely followed by a massed artillery bombardment that saw almost 800 guns throw over 30,000 shells into the city. Once the guns had done their worst, it was time for the tanks to move in. It was all going swimmingly.

Actually it wasn't. The huge bombardment had alerted the Germans to the fact that a large offensive was just around the corner and they quickly organised themselves accordingly. Also, the massed Allied tanks were meant to be advancing behind a creeping barrage but were struggling to keep up. As soon as the leading Allied tanks were inside Caen, the Germans counterattacked. The 1st SS Panzer Division and the 21st Panzer Division attacked hard and fast, and quickly regained all territory lost in the initial Allied advance. However, rocket attacks by RAF Typhoons quickly quieted the panzers down. The next day the Germans regrouped and launched another major counterattack, it too failed and by the end of 20 July Montgomery had control of Caen. He was a month late, but it didn't matter – the breakout was happening.

All along their front US troops were beginning to breakout to the south and swing round eastwards. They broke through at Avranches and fanned out to the southwest into Brittany and east towards Mortain and then back north towards Argentan. Meanwhile the British Second Army, along with their Canadian friends, continued to fight beyond Caen pushing south, threatening to hook up with their US Allies that were coming up the opposite way. Caught in the middle, facing the very real prospect of complete encirclement and probable annihilation, was the German Seventh Army.

The Allies attempted to close the gap at Falaise. To the German commanders on the ground, in the so-called Falaise Pocket, it became very clear very quickly that they were in a trap. As the Germans struggled to remove as many men as possible from the pocket before it was closed (despite Hitler's orders not to retreat) this particular part of the battlefield became one of the deadliest killing grounds of the whole war. For days on end the Germans in the pocket were smashed to pieces by Allied bombers and shell fire, and despite heroic resistance 10,000 Germans were killed and another 50,000 were taken prisoner, with thousands of burnt-out tanks and other vehicles littering the battlefield.

After the battle of the Falaise Pocket, the road to Paris opened up for the Allies.

Hitler dismissed Field Marshal von Kluge immediately. He was replaced by Field Marshal Model who was immediately ordered to withdraw to defensive positions along the Seine. The order came directly from Hitler, even though he had refused to allow von Kluge to do the exact same thing. Von Kluge took cyanide on 18 August.

Meanwhile in the East the might of the Red Army was once again on the move. It was starting to look a bit grim for the Germans.

Blitzkrieg, Red Army-style: Operation *Bagration*, 1944

The Normandy invasion was not the only Allied attack in June 1944. While thousands of men waded ashore in Northern France to give the Nazis a kicking in the West, Stalin wrote to Churchill telling him that, as agreed at the recent Tehran conference, the Russian summer offensive would kick off in mid-June at a vital part of the German eastern line. The exact area for the attack was not disclosed, Stalin would not even tell his fellow Allied leaders that level of detail.

In the East, Germany was having a rough old time of it. Army Group North had been pushed back from Leningrad while Army Group South had been kicked out of the Crimea and had also lost the vast majority of the Ukraine. Only in the centre, in Belorussia, did they continue to hold their line with any success. But the huge retreats to the north and south meant that Army Group Centre, led by Field Marshal Ernst Busch, now occupied a large salient (or bulge) in the line and was in very real danger of being encircled and trapped. It had successfully repulsed a number of Russian attacks hell bent on doing exactly that but it was surely only a matter of time before the Red Army launched something huge and unstoppable.

The Nazis knew that something was brewing in the East, but they had no clue exactly where or when it would all kick off. Hitler was convinced that Stalin would ignore the centre and continue the attack in the south. The initial Russian advances had brought them to within sniffing distance of Rumania and her valuable oil supplies and to Hitler it seemed obvious that this would be Stalin's short-term strategic goal and so made plans accordingly to meet him head on. Significant Wehrmacht reserves were moved away from Army Group Centre to Army Group South, including large numbers of panzers, which left Busch alarmingly short of armour. Despite his own intelligence telling him that he would be bearing the full force of the Russian attack, Busch didn't question the decision of his Führer.

In hindsight, this was a bit foolish.

As soon as Stavka (the Russian military intelligence organisation) got wind of the large movement of German forces to the south it cemented the Red Army's decision to attack straight down the middle. What's more the Red Army put together a huge deception plan in an effort to convince the Germans that they were correct and that the Russians were indeed going to attack in the south; fake radio traffic was distributed to give the appearance of a large build up of troops in the south and replica camps were positioned near the Ukrainian frontline. While all this was going on the Russian forces in the centre of the front were ordered to build defensive positions and to observe complete radio silence so as to not raise the alarm. Meanwhile the real reinforcements, mountains of armour, supplies, guns, men and ammunition were brought up to the Belorussian front at night. The trucks were not allowed to use their lights, instead the front and back of each vehicle was painted white, as were trees along the route. During the day everything had to be camouflaged so the Nazis couldn't see what was brewing. Russian aircraft continually flew up and down the line making sure that nothing could be seen. If they spotted any Russian reinforcement camp from the air they dropped a pennant that told the officer in charge that his camouflage wasn't good enough.

It was elaborate, it was painful and slow, but it worked. The Germans fell for it hook, line and sinker.

The Russian plan for the offensive (codenamed Operation *Bagration* after General Piotr Bagration, a Russian prince who died fighting Napoleon at Borodino in 1812) was daring and elaborate; Army Group Centre would be attacked simultaneously from the north and the south in an attempt to encircle the enemy, then the two attacking forces would join up and drive west towards Minsk – cutting off any hope of a German retreat. The plan was huge (Army Group Centre was made up of around 1 million men) and ambitious. The Russians had never tried anything like this before, but Stalin gave the nod and the plans for *Bagration* were set in action for a mid-June assault.

The scale of *Bagration* dwarfed the invasion of France in every single way. An eye-watering 2.3 million frontline and support troops would attack along a 450-mile front, backed up by over 5,000 tanks and self-propelled guns, over 10,500 heavy artillery pieces, 2,300 Katyusha multiple rocket launchers and over 5,000 aircraft. To feed the guns, tanks and men, 1.2 million tons of ammunition, rations, fuel and supplies were stockpiled behind the frontlines.

It would be the largest Allied operation of the war by a country mile.

Despite all of this the Germans were still convinced that the attack would take place in the south. Field Marshal Busch even went on leave for a few days, his timing would prove to be off slightly as in the early morning of 22 June 1944, three years to the day after Hitler launched Operation *Barbarossa*, the Red Army launched their attack. It was payback time.

The Russian guns leapt into life at 05:00hrs. Each of them had been given six tonnes of ammunition to play with during the two-hour rolling barrage which first smashed the frontline trenches and strongholds along the German frontline before moving to the rear to catch any retreating soldiers and destroy communication lines. If that little lot wasn't enough, the Katyusha rocket batteries also got in on the action. For those two hours very little would have survived in the forward zones of the German lines.

After the guns had done their worst it was time for the infantry to get in on the action, although it would not be a full-scale infantry advance. Instead small sections of mobile infantry went forward more to gather intelligence and to create openings and weak points in the line, ready for the big push the next day. That night Soviet bombers flew over 1,000 sorties in an effort to pound the German lines and keep the enemy's head well and truly down. Army Group Centre only had a handful of operational aircraft with which to respond; the Red Army had total domination of the air.

The following day saw the launch of the main Russian attack along the German central and northern fronts. In the centre of the line the attack concentrated on the German salient. The Red Army attacked the salient from all sides with huge numbers of mobile infantry with the express desire to encircle and trap as many German soldiers as possible. In the north they drove straight towards the German Third Panzer Army, based in the city of Vitebsk and under the command of General Reinhardt, a veteran of the battle for Moscow a few years earlier. It sounded formidable but in reality it was anything but. Reinhardt's 'army' had hardly any tanks left and was a shadow of its former glory. By the afternoon of the 23rd, the Third Panzer Army's line had been broken and Vitebsk was close to being completely surrounded.

Busch requested permission to retreat and get his men out of Vitebsk before it was too late, but Hitler had randomly designated Vitebsk a 'Fortified City' that was now to be held until the last man. This decision practically sealed the fate of the 28,000 German soldiers who were stationed there.

Meanwhile on 24 June the attack in the south of the salient commenced across the difficult terrain of the Pripet Marshes. Within one week the German front collapsed with the German Fourth and Ninth Armies, along with the First Panzer Army almost totally wiped off the face of the planet.

It was looking bad for Busch. Really bad. His Army Group Centre was being attacked on all fronts by an enemy far superior in both numbers and armour. On 28 June Field Marshal Walter Model replaced him. Model arrived in Minsk only to find the Red Army knocking loudly on the door to his new shiny headquarters. To make matters worse, Army Group Centre had no reserves left to counterattack Soviet bridgeheads. In just one week of brutal fighting 50,000 German soldiers were killed trying to fend off the Red Army assault on Minsk, with another 20,000 taken prisoner.

It was all in vain. Minsk fell on 4 July.

In contrast to the slow Allied progress in France, the Red Army was rampant. Over the following weeks the massive offensive continued to steamroller anything that got in its way. On 17 July thousands of captured Germans including nineteen generals, were paraded through Moscow, much to the delight of the Russian public. Meanwhile the advance continued unabated; in the south Brest-Litovsk fell on 26 July; Lvov a day later. By the end of August the Wehrmacht had been completely kicked out of Belorussia, southern Poland and a good chunk of the Baltics. In the process the German Army Group Centre had been completely destroyed. German losses are almost impossible to ascertain accurately but general consensus is that around 400,000 men were either killed, wounded or taken prisoner.

At last, Nazi Germany was fighting a two-front war in northern Europe – the dreaded scenario that Hitler had managed to avoid since 1939 – and the German people could now see the writing on the wall. It was no accident that on 20 July dissident officers tried to assassinate their Führer in a dramatic bid to make peace before Germany was ruined.

Coûte que coûte: *Valkyrie*, **1943–44**

Hitler had been the target of regular assassination attempts since he rose to power. In 1938 numerous high-ranking army officials including such people as Ludwig Beck (a former Chief of Army General Staff), Colonel General Walther von Brauchitsch (Commander in Chief of the Army) and Franz Halder (Chief of the Army General Staff) planned to overthrow Hitler in the event of war with Czechoslovakia, as it happened, the 'Munich Settlement' ended this particular little scheme, although it did make a brief re-appearance when Hitler did annex Czechoslovakia, although never gained enough ground to be a serious threat to his safety.

In the same year Swiss student Maurice Bavaud travelled to Munich specifically to shoot Hitler as he took part in the anniversary pageant of the Beer Hall Putsch but abandoned his plan when Hitler decided to march through the streets surrounded by other Nazi leaders, instead of riding in his car. Exactly one year later in the same place a German carpenter (and Communist sympathiser), Johann Georg Elser, managed to place a time bomb next to the speaking platform. The bomb exploded, killed eight people, injured another sixty-two but failed to kill or injure Hitler. In 1943 General Henning von Tresckow placed a time bomb disguised as a bottle of cognac on board Hitler's plane. Unfortunately the low temperatures in the baggage hold of the plane prevented the fuse from working and Hitler landed safely in Smolensk to visit troops in the East.

The list went on…

Beck continued to plan against Hitler in the background and once the US had entered the war following the Japanese attack at Pearl Harbor, he found many more supporters among the army officer class. One of the men he came into contact with in Berlin was a young staff officer called Claus Schenk Graf von Stauffenberg.

Stauffenberg was the son of south German aristocrats and joined the German cavalry in 1926, achieving a commission in 1930. As Hitler came to power he found himself agreeing with some of the Nazi nationalist ideologies, but he never became a member of the party. When war broke out he found himself invading Poland before his unit was reorganised and became the 6th Panzer Division; he served with distinction as a Staff Officer during the Battle of France, winning the Iron Cross First Class. At this time he, like a lot of his fellow officers, was mightily impressed at the military success of Hitler and the Wehrmacht, but then Hitler decided to invade Russia.

He was transferred to the German High Command on the Eastern Front where he met with von Tresckow who was also serving in the East. Von Tresckow was an intelligent chap and realised that the vastness and remoteness of the Eastern Front was an ideal breeding ground for a group of dissenters such as he to thrive and plot their next moves. He actively sought out like-minded officers and quickly had a small group of dedicated and influential peers who had a common aim: to kill Adolf Hitler.

In July 1941 von Tresckow tried to get von Stauffenberg in on his team, but although von Stauffenberg agreed that Hitler was a menace to Germany, he was not willing to join the band of conspirators at that moment. He was convinced Germany needed to win the war first, then deal with its leader. But as the war in the East dragged on he began to question Hitler's military leadership, he thought that a quick victory in the East was possible and it was also at about this time he started to hear rumours of terrible atrocities being carried out against Jews and gypsies in the name of Germany. The reports of genocide shocked and repulsed von Stauffenberg to such an extent that this news, coupled with the seeming inability of the senior commanders to produce a victory against Russia, turned this decent loyal officer into something of a rebel.

The battle of Stalingrad, where Hitler refused to allow any kind of strategic retreat at all, thus condemning almost an entire army to death, only added fuel to von Stauffenberg's fire – he was now utterly convinced Hitler had to go. He became so vocal about his views that his fellow officers became worried what would happen to him if the wrong person heard him rant. This may have been one of the reasons he was suddenly re-posted to Tunisia in 1943 with the 10th Panzer Division.

During his service in Tunisia von Stauffenberg was badly injured when Allied bombers attacked his motorised column. He lost his left eye, right hand and two fingers from his left hand. While recovering from his wounds in a Munich hospital he told his wife, Nina, that it was time for him to save the German Reich. He wasn't a Nazi, but he was a German patriot and keen that Germany should not be occupied or lose territory after the war. He feared that Hitler would destroy Germany and he had now decided it was time to act.

During his recovery a role as a staff officer to the headquarters of the *Ersatzheer* (Reserve Army) became vacant – von Stauffenberg claimed it quickly. It was here that he met von Tresckow again and became fully embroiled in a plan to take down the Führer once and for all.

The *Ersatzheer* offered up a unique opportunity for the conspirators as it had the power to put in place Operation *Valkyrie*: a plan approved by Hitler that would see the *Ersatzheer* fully mobilise and take control of Germany in the event of a national emergency. Once they had dealt with Hitler, the conspirators planned to use a modified version of *Valkyrie* to trick the *Ersatzheer* into mobilisation under the false pretense that the SS had killed Hitler and attempted a coup d'état.

In August and September 1943 von Tresckow started to rewrite Operation *Valkyrie*, putting in place instructions for the *Ersatzheer* to occupy key government ministries, Himmler's headquarters in East Prussia, radio stations, communications centres and other Nazi offices all over Germany. He and von Stauffenberg even went as far as drawing up the new look government for when the Nazis had been kicked out.

However, there were two tiny problems with their plan...

Firstly, only Hitler himself and General Frederick Fromm (Commander of the *Ersatzheer*) could issue the order for *Valkyrie*, this was a pain because it meant that Fromm needed to be won over somehow and included in their gang. Secondly, and this was more than a just a tiny problem if we are being honest, no one in their group had direct access to Hitler and without direct access it was going to prove very difficult to kill him.

Then, in June 1944, the assassination gods smiled upon the would-be conspirators as von Stauffenberg landed a job as chief of staff to none other than General Frederick Fromm. Not only would he now be able to quietly influence Fromm from the inside, but he would also get invites to attend Hitler's military briefings that were held either at his 'Wolf's Lair' in Rastenburg, East Prussia or at Berchtesgaden in the Bavarian Alps. These briefings would perhaps offer up the best chance to pull off the assassination.

#happydays

Time, however, was not on the conspirators' side. The Gestapo was watching them closely and several key members of the wider team were arrested. Plus, with the Allies closing in on Germany rapidly from the east and west, there was a feeling that if they didn't act quickly it would all be a bit too late. Indeed, at one point von Stauffenberg even asked von Tresckow whether they should bother going through with it, seeing as it would achieve little or no political gains. Von Tresckow responded passionately:

'The assassination must be attempted, coûte que coûte [whatever the cost]. Even if it fails, we must take action in Berlin. For the practical purpose no longer matters; what matters now is that the German resistance movement must take the plunge before the eyes of the world and of history. Compared to that, nothing else matters.'

That was that. The assassination was definitely on.

The original plan was that General Helmuth Stieff would carry out the deed on 7 July during a display of new uniforms that Hitler was going to attend at Kelssheim Castle near Salzburg. Once Hitler was dead von Stauffenberg would manage the situation in Berlin and oversee the execution of *Valkyrie*. Unfortunately Stieff bottled it at the last minute and Hitler walked away from Kelssheim Castle unharmed. Von Stauffenberg was getting increasingly frustrated and impatient and decided to plant a bomb during one of Hitler's military meetings and then hotfoot it back to Berlin to make sure everything there went to plan.

The next opportunity for von Stauffenberg was 14 July.

On that day von Stauffenberg attended a military conference hosted by his Führer at his 'Wolf's Lair' residence. He had with him a fully functioning and very explosive bomb in his briefcase, but he did not detonate it. Not because he bottled it, but because it had been agreed in advance that *Valkyrie* had the best chance to succeed if both Heinrich Himmler (leader of the SS) and Hermann Göring (leader of the Luftwaffe and nominated successor to Hitler as Führer) could be taken out at the same time. Himmler was not present at the meeting, so von Stauffenberg aborted his mission.

Twenty-four hours later, von Stauffenberg was back at the Wolf's Lair and this time with new instructions. It now didn't matter if Himmler or Göring were present. Stauffenberg was to plant his briefcase with the bomb in Hitler's conference room with a timer running, excuse himself from the meeting, wait for the big bang, then speed back to Berlin to join the other members of the conspiracy team.

Once again von Stauffenberg was forced to abort at the last minute. Hitler was called out of the meeting as the timer ticked on. Fortunately he was able to get to his briefcase and reset the timer, but it was a very close-run thing.

Over the following days, there were more rumours of Gestapo nets closing in on the plotters. They were all getting very nervous indeed and became desperate for a chance to act before it was too late. On 20 July von Stauffenberg once more jetted off to the Wolf's Lair for a military conference. Once more he had a bomb in his briefcase.

At around 11:30hrs von Stauffenberg went to Keitel's barracks for a pre-meeting briefing. He excused himself halfway through on the pretext he needed to freshen up before the meeting and nipped into a nearby washroom. There he went about arming his bombs. He had two blocks of plastic explosives, each weighing about one kilogram. The detonation system used copper chloride to eat through wire holding the firing pin. It would take ten minutes for the wire to break and lead to the firing of the explosive. Two kilograms of plastic explosives going off in a concrete bunker would cause massive destruction. It was unlikely anyone would survive.

With von Stauffenberg's injuries, priming the bombs took a long while. He was almost caught red-handed by a guard knocking at the door to tell him the meeting was about to begin. As a result he was only able to prime one of the bombs.

Another blow to the plan was that at the last minute the meeting was moved from the underground bunker to a large wooden hut due to it being a lovely summer's day. Such a building would lessen the impact of the explosion. But it was too late to worry about any of that, von Stauffenberg had to carry on with his mission.

He walked into the conference room containing Hitler and twenty other high-ranking officers of the Third Reich and placed his briefcase under the map table next to Hitler. After a few nervous minutes von Stauffenberg made his excuses and left the map room. It was 12:40hrs, and there were just a couple of minutes to go before everyone in that wooden room were blown to pieces.

As von Stauffenberg got into his staff car the bomb went off.

He managed to bluff his way out of the very heavily guarded Wolf's Lair and by 13:15hrs he was on a plane back to Berlin convinced that Hitler was dead.

Only he wasn't.

Shortly after von Stauffenberg left the room, someone (most probably Colonel Heinz Brandt who was standing next to Hitler) kicked the briefcase behind the leg of conference table. This seemingly unconscious act would ultimately save the life of his Führer. The table leg shielded most people, including Hitler, from the worst of the blast. Only four people were killed. Hitler suffered wounds to his legs and a perforated eardrum. His trousers were ruined. However, he was ultimately OK; in fact three hours later he was giving Mussolini a quick tour of the bomb site.

By the time von Stauffenberg landed back in Berlin his fellow plotters had already had a phone call from General Erich Fellgiebel, an officer at the *Wolfsschanze* (Wolf's Lair – Hitler's Eastern Front compound) who was in on the ruse, to tell them the bad news. As a result Operation *Valkyrie* was not initiated. However, as soon as he landed von Stauffenberg phoned in from the airport to triumphantly announce that the bomb had exploded successfully and the Führer was dead. Confusion reigned. No one knew who to believe.

Finally at about 16:00hrs the order for Operation *Valkyrie* was given. In many places the coup went ahead with regional leaders ordering the arrests of local SS leaders. The only leading Nazi in Berlin at the time was Joseph Goebbels. Otto Remer, a major in the Guards Battalion and a fanatical Nazi, was sent to arrest him. Goebbels immediately got Hitler on the phone to prove he was still alive. Remer was promoted on the spot to colonel and then ordered to hunt down the conspirators.

The coup was not going well.

Himmler issued a counter-order and slowly began to regain control over the situation, he was helped by the fact that Hitler himself made a few personal phone calls during the evening to prove to his staff that he was alive.

Operation *Valkyrie* was dead.

Fromm, perhaps in an effort to cover up the fact he knew about the plot, arrested von Stauffenberg, Olbricht and two other members of the conspiracy and via a farcical court martial process made up of just himself, successfully sentenced them all to death by firing squad. At ten minutes past midnight they were all shot in the courtyard outside the War Ministry. Dead men wouldn't be able to grass him up. That same day von Tresckow committed suicide on the Eastern Front.

To say that Hitler was furious about the whole thing is an epic understatement. He was incandescent. He ordered the Gestapo to hunt down everyone who had been even the slightest bit involved in any tiny part of the plot to kill him. And once they had found them all, they were to round up all of their families too. The Gestapo, being the Gestapo, carried out this task with relish, they even took the opportunity to settle some old scores in the process, arresting people who had no involvement in the bomb plot but had annoyed them in some other way over the last few years. In all over 7,000 people were arrested. 4,980 were executed.

The assassination attempt did not topple the Nazi regime as planned, in fact the Nazis increased their control over almost all aspects of German life. In the eyes of many Germans, it had gone from bad to worse.

The Champagne Campaign: Operation *Dragoon* and the Liberation of France, 1944

While the Allied top brass were busy planning *Overlord*, they decided that a smaller landing, initially codenamed Operation *Anvil*, should be made in southern France at the same time. However as time ticked on towards D-Day Eisenhower became nervous that *Anvil* might take precious landing craft and men away from the main attack in Normandy. So, *Anvil* was postponed.

Once President Roosevelt had witnessed the success of *Overlord* he resurrected the idea of a second invasion of France. By now it had a new codename – *Dragoon* – and it would use men and materials diverted from Italy. Churchill was not best pleased, he didn't want to weaken the Italian front and instead preferred an attack in the Balkans. He thought that an attack in this area would capture vital Nazi oil and petrol reserves and would also check the advance of Russia, thus giving him better bargaining power in the post-war power struggle that was bound to materialise.

Roosevelt wasn't having any of it though, and plans for *Dragoon* carried on at pace. On 14 July 1944 the invasion plan was ratified by the Allied Combined Chiefs of Staff and the date of 15 August 1944 was put in the diary.

The main primary objective for *Dragoon* was to capture the important French ports of Marseille and Toulon. Having these two ports in Allied pockets would help enormously with the task of supplying an ever-growing Allied army in France. It was also hoped that a further invasion to the south would stop any more German reinforcements being transferred to Normandy and squeeze the rest of the Nazis out of France for good.

On 13 August the Allies launched an all-out air assault along the Mediterranean coastline. For the next forty-eight hours they softened up the enemy by smashing communications links, coastal defences and transportation hubs in preparations for the landings, which were due to hit the sands on 15 August 1944. Over 1,000 vessels, including five battleships, placed the US Seventh Army and the French Army B onto the beaches of southern France between St Raphael and Le Lavandou, close to Monaco and the Italian border along the French Riviera. The landings took place right under the noses of the German Nineteenth Army, part of Colonel-General von Blaskowitz's Army Group G.

Thanks to a massive naval bombardment which threw over 50,000 shells onto the coastal defence systems of the invasion beaches, and air support which effectively kept the Luftwaffe well away from the action, the men landed largely unopposed. Near Saint Tropez, as the men leapt ashore they were met, not by enemy machine-guns or artillery fire, but by a little French chap who appeared out of the mist carrying a tray of champagne glasses.

From that moment on the landings were known as the *Champagne Campaign*.

By the end of that first day the Allies had safely put ashore over 60,000 men, 6,000 vehicles and 50,000 tonnes of supplies with the loss of just 320 men. Compared to Normandy it was a walk in the park.

Breakout from the beachheads was also rapid. Within twenty-four hours of initial touchdown on French sand the Americans had liberated a number of coastal towns and had managed to push inland across a broad front. A second wave of men landed on the beaches on the 16th – among them four divisions of French colonial troops, plus the French 1st Armoured Division. These French soldiers set about the task of liberating their homeland with gusto and enthusiasm and made rapid progress. Allied movement was so fast and so decisive that Hitler agreed to a general evacuation of south and southeast France, ordering Field Marshal Model's Army Group B to hold a defensive line to the south of Paris and on to Switzerland, although the ports of Toulon and Marseilles were to be held 'at all costs' and 'defended to the last man'. These were orders that were nearly taken literally.

The fighting for both Marseilles and Toulon during the last week of August 1944 was ferocious, almost Verdun-esque in its brutality. In Toulon the French troops took more than 17,000 German prisoners as they finally wrestled the town out of German hands. It cost almost 3,000 French lives to do so. At virtually the same time, another fierce fight was raging in Marseilles with Algerian and Moroccan troops forcing the German garrison to surrender on the 28th. Although the installations and equipment at both ports were smashed to bits by the Germans, the French were proud of the fact that they had kicked the Nazis out of the south of France a month ahead of schedule.

Magnifique!

In the north, the breakout from Normandy was gathering some serious pace. By the night of 19/20 August General Patton's Third US Army had crossed the Seine and were less than forty miles from Paris.

In the original invasion plan Paris was not actually identified as a priority. Eisenhower wanted to concentrate on pushing the Germans out of France; he thought that by doing this the Nazis would leave the capital by their own accord anyhow. However, once the Parisian population got wind of the American advance, they took matters into their own hands and attempted to overthrow the enemy themselves. In the chaos the police went on strike and things threatened to get very much out of hand. Reluctantly, to try and save a potentially dangerous situation, Eisenhower agreed to let French troops have a go at liberating the city.

The French 2nd Armoured Division was let loose on Paris. The fought long and hard along the approach roads to the city, losing over 300 men and forty tanks along the way. The Germans were not giving up without a fight, but by 24 August French tanks were rolling through the centre of Paris. The following day the German garrison surrendered.

Paris was free.

The following day General de Gaulle entered Paris amid scenes of wild celebration. He rekindled the flame on the tomb of the unknown soldier at the Arc de Triomphe and then marched at the head of the liberating forces down the Champs Élysées. Meanwhile Hitler flew into a rage of epic proportions. He had issued explicit instructions that Paris was only to be handed back to the Allies as a heap of rubble and was not impressed. On the 26th Hitler's chief of staff, Alfred Jodl, called up Field Marshal Model with an order to smash Paris to pieces immediately with V-1 rockets and the army's massive siege mortars. Model wasn't in the office and instead General Hans Speidel answered the phone.

Speidel decided not to pass on the message to his boss.

By early September Montgomery had marched into Belgium and Luxembourg and was itching to carry on the advance to the Rhine. There was literally nothing to stop him, but he was given the order to pause to enable supply lines to catch up with his rapid advance. The same story was true for General Patton who had liberated Nancy and had his eye on Metz and beyond – straight into the heart of Germany. Despite repeated attempts to lobby Eisenhower for more fuel he was told in no uncertain terms to hold his horses and wait. It was very frustrating for all involved.

The pause in the advance gave the Germans a chance to regroup slightly and once the Allies were allowed back on the march, they found themselves fighting rather than chasing the enemy. As the advance bogged down in Holland plans were being hatched for an attack on a Dutch city positioned on the banks of the Neder Rijn (the Dutch stretch of the Rhine) which, if taken would open up a clear path to the Ruhr.

That city was called Arnhem.

90 Per Cent Successful: Arnhem, 1944

During September 1944 Montgomery became frustrated with his progress. Appalling weather and a shortage of fuel and supplies meant his rapid advance through France and Belgium had ground to a halt. The sluggishness of the advance had also allowed the enemy time to reorganise themselves and the Allies' progress was now not only slow, it was violent.

Monty was convinced that the northern end of the Siegfried Line was there for the taking. The Germans had a very long front to defend in the West and this part of the line seemed weak – a concentrated attack here, Monty argued, would crush the Nazi defenses easily. All he needed to put this in place was control over the bridges that crossed the Rhine (which he would capture using a large airborne assault) and then his armour could be on its merry way straight into the Ruhr area of Germany – the industrial beating heart of the Reich – thus pulling the plug on German weapons production. If successful, Montgomery was convinced that the war could be done and dusted by Christmas 1944.

It was ambitious and a little bit reckless – dropping thousands of men behind enemy lines was obviously dangerous, but this plan also meant that the area around Antwerp would still be in German hands – but Eisenhower somehow approved it on 10 September.

Operation *Market Garden* (as the assault was codenamed) was all systems go.

The plan for *Market Garden* looked relatively simple (on paper at least). Three airborne divisions would be allocated to occupy different sections of the waterways. The US 82nd Airborne Division was given the task of taking the Grave bridge over the River Maas and another smaller bridge over the River Waal at Nijmegen. The US 101st Airborne Division was to overrun the small enemy garrison at Eindhoven and capture the bridges that spanned the Wilhelmina Canal, the Dommel and the Wilhelms Canal, and finally the British 1st Airborne Division was pencilled in to take the bridges over the Nederrijn at Arnhem, establish a bridgehead around the town and await reinforcements from the Polish 1st Parachute Brigade and the British 52nd (Airportable) Division. If all objectives were met and all the bridges captured, the airborne troops would have opened up a corridor along which Lieutenant General Horrocks's British XXX Corps would advance, linking up with the American airborne units before relieving the British at Arnhem and heading off towards Germany.

Dropping that many men behind enemy lines was audacious and daring. If the plan was to succeed it needed everything to go like clockwork. Lieutenant General Browning would be Montgomery's top man on the ground during the operation and he was nervous. His opinion was that his men could hold on to the bridges for no more than four days without reinforcements. Horrocks had to make it on time. The main problem with an airborne assault was the attacking forces could only carry with them a limited amount of weaponry and supplies. They were dependent on ground forces helping them out quickly, otherwise the men were very susceptible to counterattacks from enemy tanks and heavy guns.

And, unfortunately for Montgomery, Browning's nerves were merited.

The airborne drop was scheduled for 17 September 1944. General Browning could only scrape together 1,600 gliders which wasn't anywhere near enough to drop 10,000 men onto the bridges in one go, three waves were needed which gave commanders on the ground and in the air their first headache of the assault – the second and third waves needed to be dropped with pinpoint accuracy to enable them to reinforce the first wave.

Another headache for the top brass was the fact that in many cases the paratroopers had to be dropped several miles away from the targets in order for them to land on safe ground, this gave the defending Germans ample warning to get their act together. Not surprisingly the results of the first wave were decidedly mixed. The US 101st Airborne under General

Maxwell Taylor secured virtually all their objectives in short order except for one bridge over the Wilhelmina Canal, which was demolished before they could arrive. Their mates in the 82nd Airborne initially made good progress too and quickly captured the Grave bridge, but were eventually held up at the vital road bridge at Nijmegen by strong German resistance. All in all the Americans weren't doing too bad.

The British 1st Airborne had a slightly less effective start however.

Because the town of Arnhem was bristling with anti-aircraft defences the British paratroopers were forced to land in rough scrubland over seven miles from the bridges they were meant to capture. Radio communications were poor at best and progress was slow, chaotic and costly. By evening only one out of the three British paratroop regiments had managed to get to the Arnhem Road Bridge. About 500 men led by Lieutenant Colonel John Frost had managed to capture one side of the bridge but they were pinned down, surrounded and in all sorts of trouble.

Then, to make matters even worse, the panzers turned up.

Montgomery knew that there were panzer units in the area, but he had discounted them because his information led him to believe they were being refitted and, as such, out of action. He was sadly mistaken. Not only were they very ready for a fight (albeit not at full strength) they just happened to be the elite 9th and 10th SS Panzer Divisions.

Field Marshal Model watched the thousands of paratroopers gently fall from the sky around Arnhem and quickly dispatched his two panzer divisions towards the town, one on either side of the river. The British paras (and General Horrocks) were about to get the shock of their lives.

At the same time as the paras were dropping in on the Germans from the air, General Horrocks and his XXX Corps began its armoured thrust to meet up with the airborne troops. By the 19th a forward detachment of the XXX Corps had reached, repaired and crossed the Son bridge that had been destroyed over the Wilhelmina Canal and later that evening the main body of XXX Corps reached Nijmegen, but it took another day of brutal fighting to get across the River Waal. In the end Allied troops had to paddle across the river in small boats in full view of the enemy in an effort to capture the bridge.

Meanwhile the British men clinging on to one side of the bridge at Arnhem had been there for three days and were getting desperate. Major Blackwood of the 4th Parachute Brigade summed up the situation:

'Message to say that our attack on the Arnhem bridge had been beaten back and that German tanks had outflanked and surrounded us… Our orders were brief – wait for the tanks, give them everything we had in the way of grenades, shoot up as many infantry as we could before we died.'

By 21 September Colonel Frost had been wounded. He had just one hundred men left. Not surprisingly they were overrun and captured. Despite reinforcements being dropped in in the shape of determined Polish paratroopers the Germans now controlled the entire crossing at Arnhem. With the panzers flexing their muscles and the hope of capturing the bridge gone, the remnants of the British 1st Airborne now concentrated all of their efforts on getting out of the inferno alive. Meanwhile the XXX Corps were being shot to pieces as they tried desperately to reach Arnhem from the Waal – they were in very real danger of being completely encircled.

General Browning had no choice but to cancel the operation on 25 September.

Of the 10,000 men who were dropped into the battle, only 2,163 made it back in one piece. Over 1,200 men had been killed with some 6,000 herded into captivity. Casualties for the British XXX Corps were around 1,500.

Montgomery famously said that the operation was '90 per cent successful' and in a way he was correct because most of the bridges were captured. However the vital crossing at Arnhem stayed in German possession and without it the Allies could not carry out their plan.

The war would not be over by Christmas.

Vergeltungswaffe: Flying bombs, 1943–44

From 1942 onwards Hitler bored the pants off of anyone who would listen about how the war would be won by Germany's secret weapons, against which the Allies would have no defence. Many members of his staff thought he was a bit crazy especially as the months passed by without sight or sound of any of these so-called game changers. Yet, out of sight of all but a chosen few, progress on a number of highly advanced weapons was steadily being made, with the first experimental firing of a V-2 rocket taking place on 13 June 1942. The V stood for *Vergeltungswaffe* (German for vengeance weapon).

That first test wasn't particularly successful, with the rocket crashing out of control soon after take-off and almost killing Albert Speer, the German Minister for Armaments, and a very interested spectator. Further tests were carried out on 14 October 1942 and they were much more successful, a delighted Speer told Hitler the good news and very soon the order was signed for their mass production.

By the beginning of the 1943 there were rumours flying around the Allied corridors of power that the Nazis were planning a new range of special weapons and in May that year Allied surveillance had pinpointed several construction sites that they were convinced were being built for rocket-powered weapons, including a secret base at Peenemünde Airfield. Churchill was so worried about it that he authorised a huge bombing raid on Peenemünde, which took place during the night of 17 August 1943. 596 bombers dropped almost 2,000 tonnes of high explosive bombs on the facility and although not massively successful (V-weapon production was only delayed by a matter of weeks) this raid heralded the beginning of sustained campaign of bombing codenamed Operation *Crossbow* which reached its height during summer of 1944 when 60,000 tonnes of explosives were dropped on V-1 production sites.

Meanwhile Allied intelligence was being significantly enhanced by the brave work carried out by the Polish Resistance. Constant information was being sent back to London about manufacturing and research sites throughout Europe, which helped greatly in directing the ongoing bombing raids. However, the Polish outdid themselves when they came across a complete V1 rocket that had landed in the River Bug and failed to explode. At enormous risk the Poles removed the wings so that the Germans couldn't locate their rocket and then, when it was safe, Polish engineers went back to the site, recovered the bomb and smuggled it in small pieces back to Warsaw. Eventually the weapon was flown to England and as a result Allied scientists knew what the weapon could do and what it couldn't do. What they didn't know was what would Hitler do with it and when would he start?

The fact is that the *Vergeltungswaffe* project was late. Late because those pesky bombers from the RAF and USAAF (United States Army Air Force) kept smashing production facilities and because producing new technology such as this was bound to take longer than any warlord would want. In the end it wasn't until after the D-Day landings that the first V-1 weapon was launched against London. On 13 June 1944 three V-1 rockets reached London. Two exploded harmlessly away from any civilians but the other one landed in the middle of the East End and killed six people.

Forty-eight hours later the Germans had another go at smashing London to pieces. 244 V-1 flying bombs were launched at London in just twenty-four hours with seventy-two exploding and causing damage. Throughout June every part of London had a piece of V-1 action although much of this was more luck than judgement on the part of Germany – the aiming of the V-1 was crude to say the least with error ranges of up to fifteen miles all too common. A lot of the bombs fell short, which meant the south-eastern suburbs of London got more than their fair share of V-1 treatment. Croydon was especially roughed up with seventy-five per cent of the borough's homes damaged or destroyed.

Defending London from these flying bombs was tricky business. Anti-aircraft gunners tried valiantly, however shooting down a bomb over London only helped the Germans out. The V-1 had a top speed of over

400 mph, which was faster than all available Allied fighters except the brand new Hawker Tempest V which could hit 436 mph. Allied pilots soon discovered that trying to shoot a V-1 out of the sky was both difficult and dangerous. The V-1 was tiny and in order to have a fair chance of shooting it pilots had to get within 200 yards of the bomb, at this close range if they hit their target the resulting explosion would almost certainly take them out too. Another option was for the pilots to try and fly next to the bombs and either physically tip the bomb over using the wing of their aircraft and send it crashing into the sea or get close enough to disturb the airflow over the bomb's wings which would end in the same result. Either option was pretty dangerous and with large numbers of V-1 rockets crossing the North Sea every day, it was not a viable long-term strategy.

By 6 July 1944, 2,754 bombs had been launched against London resulting in 2,752 casualties. Something needed to be done. Quickly.

The men behind the *Crossbow* campaign decided to move the bulk of London's anti-aircraft defence system to the coast, they also started to use new proximity-fused shells which exploded when they got near to their target – they couldn't be used over land, but they proved to be quite effective shooting out to sea. In four days 1,000 anti-aircraft guns and 23,000 personnel were relocated to new positions. The relocation worked, by the end of August only one V-1 in seven was getting through to London and with the Allied armies fast marching eastwards in France V-1 launch sites were quickly located and destroyed – massed V-1 attacks were now a thing of the past although the odd long-range rocket was launched from deep inside Holland right up until the end of the war.

However, if the Allies thought that London was now safe from Nazi nastiness they were badly mistaken. Hitler and his scientists were ready to unleash another vengeance weapon. Bigger, badder and more bloodthirsty than the V-1 – the so-called V-2 rocket was a monster.

The V-2 weighed about twelve tonnes, carried a tonne of explosives and had a range of 200 miles. The kicker with the V-2 was that it could hit speeds of up to 4,000 mph meaning that nothing apart from technical malfunction could stop it reaching its target. It was the world's first ballistic missile and the first man-made object to make a sub-orbital space flight. Also, although it packed only slightly more explosives than the V-1, the incredible speed at which it hit the ground greatly magnified its destructive effect. Civilians below had little or no warning as to the incoming disaster.

The first V-2 rockets arrived in London on 8 September 1944.

By that time the Nazi war machine was churning out over 600 V-2 rockets per month and over 1,400 rockets were fired at England between 8 September and 27 March 1945, London got the vast majority of these, but other cities such as Norwich and Ipswich also had visits by the V-2. More than half of these fell short but the 500 or so that did get through killed 2,754 civilians, injuring 6,476 more. However, this was nothing compared to the treatment dished out to the Dutch city of Antwerp.

In total Antwerp received 8,696 V-1 bomb visits and 1,610 V-2 bomb visits. It was given special treatment after it fell into Allied hands due to its importance as a supply hub to the advancing Allied armies. 3,470 Belgian civilians were killed along with 682 Allied soldiers.

As well as the V-1 and V-2 there were other weapons bubbling away on the Nazi production line but they didn't see active service. The V-3 was a long-range gun designed to fire a shell almost 100 miles but was abandoned when the two designated target sites near Calais were destroyed by Allied bombers. The V-4 was a ground to air missile that was close to production in 1944 but didn't have enough support from Hitler to make it a reality.

Although they killed and maimed many thousands of people, ultimately Hitler's revenge weapons failed to turn the tide of the war and it could be argued consumed huge amounts of brainpower and resources that perhaps could have gone into improving and manufacturing thousands more tanks, planes and guns that may well have had a material impact on the actual fighting.

MacArthur returns: Triumph in the Philippines, 1994

As the Allied advance through France gathered pace, the Americans in the Pacific were fighting among themselves as to what move to make next. General MacArthur was desperate to make good on his promise to return to the Philippines but the majority of the US Navy top brass wanted to leap-frog the Philippines and head straight for the Japanese home islands. The discussions were energetic and intense, but in the end MacArthur won – they would invade the Philippines on 20 October 1944.

Before the main push on the Philippines the Americans made a concerted effort to limit Japanese ability to respond and throw reinforcements into the fight.

The invasion fleet, under the watchful eye of Vice-Admiral Thomas Kinkaid, arrived on the scene on 17 October with 174,000 men of the US Sixth Army. The island of Leyte, in the more weakly defended central area of the islands, was chosen as the starting point for the invasion and over the next forty-eight hours the US Navy duly proceeded to smash the coastal defences to smithereens in preparation for the men to wade ashore.

As it turned out the island was only lightly defended by a single Japanese division. The US Sixth Army poured onto the beaches during 20 October practically unmolested and by the evening they had managed to secure a substantial bridgehead along a seventeen-mile front. General MacArthur himself landed during the day. As the would-be liberators pushed forwards, the Japanese were getting themselves organised for a massive counterattack; not on land, but in the Gulf of Leyte.

The Japanese naval high command, under Admiral Soemu Toyoda, had hatched a plan that they were convinced would deal the final decisive blow to the US fleet. The plan involved offering up the carrier task force of Vice-Admiral Ozawa as a floating sacrificial lamb to the powerful US Third Fleet under Admiral Halsey. If Halsey took the bait it would leave the landing zones of Leyte virtually defenseless and allow the central and southern Japanese naval groups (headed by Vice Admiral Takeo Kurita and Vice Admiral Kiyohide Shima respectively) to sail up undetected either side of Leyte to attack and destroy the American landings in a massive pincer movement.

It was a plan that was hugely audacious and more than a little bit crazy. It was also a plan that resulted in the greatest naval battle the world had ever seen.

The plan started off badly for the Japanese as both the southern and central naval groups were spotted and attacked to such an extent that Shima was forced to withdraw from the battle, leaving Kurita to attack the American landing zones with only one arm of the pincer. Kurita was getting pounded from the air – Halsey's aircraft made more than 250 sorties against Kurita's force during the afternoon of 24 October, sinking one battleship and damaging several other vessels. However, he cut this attack short when he heard news that his planes had spotted Ozawa's carrier fleet. Thinking that he had done enough damage to Kurita's force he immediately ordered the bulk of his task force to head straight for them and get ready for a scrap.

Kurita dusted himself down and once more set out towards the American landing zones at Leyte. There was only a scratch US detachment defending the area with some 500 aircraft and in the early morning of 25 October they engaged Kurita's Central Force, sinking two cruisers and damaging another. Despite these early victories the American situation was seemingly hopeless. They were massively outnumbered and outgunned, it was surely just a matter of time before the US Task Force at Leyte would be defeated giving the Japanese a clear run at the landing zones and beachheads. The American commanders tried to confuse their enemy by laying smoke, but there was no denying that they were smack in the middle of a crisis. Frantic messages were being sent out to Halsey to turn around and help out. If the firepower of the Japanese guns wasn't enough, Kurita also launched Kamikaze raids where pilots flew suicide missions in planes loaded with explosives directly into the superstructure of the Allied ships. These were the first recorded Kamikaze raids of the war and resulted in the sinking of the escort carrier *St. Lo* as well as damaging five other vessels.

Then, inexplicably, at 09:30hrs, the Japanese ships suddenly stopped firing, turned tail and retreated.

The Battle of Leyte Gulf was the greatest naval battle of all time if measured by tonnage with just over three million tonnes of naval firepower involved, although the Battle of Jutland boasted ten more ships at 254. Japanese losses at Leyte Gulf were eye-watering: 10,500 men and twenty-eight warships in all, compared to the US losses of just six ships.

With total sea and air superiority, the path to ultimate victory in the Philippines was well and truly open.

Back on the island of Leyte the invasion force continued to consolidate. General MacArthur made an emotional broadcast to the people of the Philippines announcing his return and urging them to help his men rid their homeland of the Japanese enemy. By the beginning of November the US Sixth Army had captured all available coastal airstrips and by Christmas Day effective Japanese resistance on the island of Leyte had ceased to exist. It had been a costly fight though with over 15,000 American casualties including 3,500 killed.

On 15 December, whilst the fighting was still continuing on Leyte, MacArthur launched the invasion of the island of Mindoro with the express order of building two air strips for the assault on Luzon (the main island in the Philippines).

Luzon was home to 250,000 Japanese soldiers commanded by General Yamashita. On paper this was a formidable force, but he had only a handful of operational planes and due to the recent naval defeat in the Leyte Gulf he had no way of easily receiving reinforcements. In contrast the US Sixth Army that was facing them measured 200,000 strong and had more men in reserve, plus they had the backing of the US Navy's Seventh Fleet of 850 ships – a sizeable advantage in anyone's book.

On 2 January 1945 part of the American Seventh Naval Fleet set sail for Luzon in order to commence the preliminary bombardment of the chosen landing zones. They were greeted by wave after wave of Kamikaze attacks, which over the next few days caused all sorts of damage and mayhem. Dozens of ships were hit, including two battleships, five cruisers and five destroyers. Eventually the attacks subsided and on 7 January the naval guns opened fire to smash the Luzon coastline. For three days the shells roared and bombs fell onto the invasion areas and on 9 January the men of the US Sixth Army waded ashore, anticipating their hottest reception yet in this Philippines campaign.

But there wasn't a single Japanese soldier in sight.

Yamashita has decided not to take the fight to the Americans on the beaches, instead he had withdrawn his men to the high ground inland. As a result the American invasion force was able to get ashore easily and establish a decent beachhead. By nightfall they had secured an area seventeen miles wide and up to four miles deep in places. Not a bad day's work to be honest.

After the landings, progress inland continued to be swift and relatively painless and by the end of January they were loudly knocking on the door of the capital Manila. Here the advance ground to a brutal standstill. The Japanese garrison that had barricaded themselves up in Manila decided to fight to the death and proved a fierce and stubborn foe. The fighting was brutal and bloody and it took a terrible toll on the civilian population who were forced to stay put in the city and were often on the receiving end of Japanese cruelty. The fight for Manila lasted until 3 March by which time the Japanese forces within the city were all but annihilated. At the close of the battle, 16,000 Japanese soldiers lay dead in the streets alongside 1,000 American soldiers and around 100,000 Filipino civilians.

Once Manila was in Allied hands the US invasion force continued to occupy the rest of the islands. Dozens of separate seaborne landings were made in an attempt to clear the southern and central islands as Japanese garrisons were pinpointed and eradicated one-by-one. It was a slow and painful job due to the tens of thousands of Japanese troops that were still hiding out in the mountains and many remained embedded right through to the final weeks of the war.

In the retaking of the Philippines the US forces lost 10,381 men killed, with a further 36,631 wounded and over 93,000 men taken sick.

Bold, Brash and Bloody: The Battle of the Bulge, 1944–45

In mid-October 1944 Eisenhower issued new orders to his top men advancing towards Germany. Montgomery was to capture Antwerp and, once successful, advance from the Maas onto the Rhine. General Omar Bradley and the US First Army was ordered to march on Cologne, while General Jacob Devers and his US Sixth Army were asked to close up on the Rhine in the south. The route to Cologne was tough. Really tough. The Germans were not giving an inch, especially in the fighting around Aachen (the first significant German town to be captured) and the Hürtgen Forest, where the fighting was especially brutal. The Nazis were scrapping for every metre of Europe – it was a hard, slow slog.

Meanwhile, in his mountain retreat, Hitler was plotting the mother of all counterattacks. A counterattack that would not only halt the Allied advance in the West, but turn it around and push the Allies back so fiercely that they would be forced to sue for peace. Such negotiations would allow Germany breathing space to transfer men and equipment to the East and stop the Russian advance on the Fatherland.

The plan was brash and adventurous, and a number of German military big-hitters such as von Rundstedt and Model thought it way too ambitious to have a hope of success. Not surprisingly Hitler ignored them all and went ahead with it anyway. He transferred thousands of men from the Eastern Front, lowered the age of conscription to sixteen-and-a-half and recruited those that had up until then been allowed to miss out on armed service due to their civilian occupation. It was all hands to the pump. The Wehrmacht numbers in the West were boosted by the tune of 700,000 new men in a matter of months.

It was game on.

Originally codenamed 'Watch on the Rhine' in an effort to fool the Allies into thinking it was a defensive action; the actual plan was anything but defensive. Two massive panzer armies would smash through the

Ardennes in a repeat of the initial moves of the 1940 invasion of France. Once through the Ardennes, they would cross the River Meuse and push north to the coast, recapture Antwerp and split the Allies in two, forcing them into another 'Dunkirk'. Such a massive offensive ran the risk of overstretching supply lines and of exposing long vulnerable flanks to Allied counterattack. Don't forget that the Allies were much stronger than the Wehrmacht in practically every department and they had complete air superiority. Success would be based on speed, surprise and poor weather, which would limit the effectiveness of the RAF and USAAF.

Preparations took place in the utmost secrecy with total radio silence. Allied intelligence had a couple of sniffs that suggested something was being plotted but they didn't have any details. The Allied top brass were convinced that the Nazis had nothing left, that they were empty and incapable of launching any kind of substantial offensive. To Eisenhower and his band of merry men, the only questions to be answered were where and when to launch the assault on the Rhine.

They were mistaken. On 16 December, after a short, sharp pre-dawn artillery barrage, the first wave of German attackers set off through thick fog. There were about half-a-million Wehrmacht troops ready to advance through the Ardennes. On the other side of the wire stood little more than 80,000 Allied troops. It seemed like May 1940 all over again.

Surprise was total. The first waves of German troops completely overran the Allied frontline. At the pointy end of the attack was the 150th Panzer Brigade – a unit of some 2,000 English-speaking German commandos who wore captured American uniforms and drove around in US Army Jeeps. They advanced deep into enemy territory causing chaos, cutting telephone wires, turning signposts, creating false minefields and setting booby-traps. If caught, they were under orders to tell their captors there were thousands of Germans roaming around in American uniforms – causing utter panic among the American forces in this sector and many a GI was arrested for not remembering their passwords or carrying ID.

As the day wore on the resemblance to May 1940 grew; the overwhelming German advance, the frightening speed of the attack and above all the chaos in the Allied rear, where bewildered men ran for safety, clogging the roads and preventing reinforcements from arriving. Within twenty-four hours the US 106th Division were surrounded and some 7,000 American soldiers surrendered. It was the largest mass surrender of American arms in the European campaign.

Over the next week or so the German war machine pushed on. The Sixth Panzer Army almost caught up with US First Army headquarters at Spa, and in the south Bastogne had been surrounded and bypassed as the Wehrmacht smashed their way towards the Meuse. As the gravity of the situation became clear to Eisenhower, he ordered all other fighting on the Western Front to stop so he could concentrate his forces on pushing back the German advance. He ordered General Patton to swing his Third Army north to attack the southern section of the 'bulge' in the American line. Montgomery took control of the northern section and got busy organising a strike on the northern edge of the bulge.

At its peak the bulge was around forty miles wide and between sixty and seventy miles deep; the Germans managed to get within three miles of the River Meuse. Supply lines were stretched and they were running out of fuel, but although they were still seventy-odd miles from Antwerp the Germans were über confident of ultimate victory.

Then, on Christmas Eve, the weather cleared.

The better weather meant that British and American fighters and fighter bombers were finally able to take to the air and boy did they make up for lost time. Thousands of sorties were flown over the next couple of days. Stricken panzers were sitting ducks as they ran out of fuel and although Hitler did eventually allow reinforcements, they lacked the fuel to make a difference to the battle.

Now, with the German advance on its knees the Americans from the south and the British from the north pressed down on the bulge to such an extent that there was a great danger of another huge encirclement à la Falaise. Von Rundstedt asked Hitler for permission to withdraw and save the men – he refused at first but by 8 January 1945, with the noose tightening around the bulge by the hour, he eventually agreed.

By 7 February the German forces were back where they had started. Hitler's big gamble in the West had failed. Big time. Casualty numbers vary greatly depending on who you believe, but it is thought that the Wehrmacht lost around 90,000 men (killed / missing / wounded / captured) along with hundreds of tanks, big guns and planes. The Allies took a similar level of beating with over 90,000 casualties all in and almost 20,000 killed.

If this loss in the West wasn't bad enough for Hitler, in the East the Russians went on the attack again, launching a strike aimed at conquering East Prussia, Prussia and, ultimately, Berlin.

A Farce in the East: Russia Advances (again), 1944–45

In December 1944 German military intelligence (Abwehr) had warned Hitler about a serious build-up of Russian armour and resources, particularly near the Vistula River that posed a real threat to East Prussia. Colonel General Heinz Guderian, Chief of the General Staff of the Army, agreed and was not shy in telling Hitler that the greatest danger to the Fatherland was a massive Russian offensive through East Prussia, Poland and ultimately into Germany.

Hitler was having none of it.

The Führer politely disagreed, believing that all of the evidence pertaining to mass Soviet troop activity in the East was nothing more than propaganda. Despite this rebuttal, Guderian presented Hitler with a detailed plan on 9 January 1945 for a strategic withdrawal in the East to more defensible positions. Hitler went crazy, threatening to lock up Major General Gehlen (head of German military intelligence) in a lunatic asylum. Three days later Guderian was probably wishing he could put someone else in that lunatic asylum.

When the Red Army launched their attack on 12 January they had over 2 million men, over 30,000 guns, 7,000-odd tanks and 5,000 planes to chuck at a German defensive line that numbered about a million men, just over 1,500 tanks and a few hundred planes. It would not be a fair fight.

Originally the attack was scheduled for 20 January but urgent appeals from Churchill for Stalin to help take the heat off of the fight in the West resulted in it being brought forward by eight days.

The attack began at 03:00hrs with a monumental artillery barrage followed by a brief dummy attack in an effort to bait the panzer units into revealing their positions. A few hours later the real offensive got started in the south on the Ukrainian front with no less than thirty-four infantry divisions marching forwards backed up by over 1,000 tanks. They completely overran the Fourth Panzer Army that was facing them and carried on another fifteen miles. Hitler was the only person who could authorise the mobilisation of reserves and he was famous for sleeping into the afternoon. By the time he was awake and had had breakfast the decisions about bringing up reinforcements were immaterial.

The Red Army was raging forth.

The story was the same in the north two days later when Marshal Zhukov's First Belorussian Army completely outnumbered and overwhelmed three German divisions, almost wiping out the German Ninth Army. Further north still the Second Belorussian Army met stiff resistance, led by the elite *SS Grossdeutschland* Panzer Corps who made thirty-seven separate counterattacks on 14 January. It was clear to everyone that the *SS Grossdeutschland* Panzer Corps was key to keeping the Second Belorussian Army out of Germany.

Clear to everyone except Hitler.

The all-seeing Führer immediately ordered them to be transferred to Poznan to deflect the Russian attack there, despite vociferous objections from Guderian and despite the fact that they would not arrive in Poznan early enough to be of any use. These facts didn't seem to matter; the *SS Grossdeutschland Panzer* Corps were pulled out of the line on 16 January.

Four days later the Russians crossed into East Prussia.

The northern flank of the Red Army (the Second Belorussian Army) turned north towards the Baltic coast. On 21 January they encircled 350,000 men of the German Fourth Army at Lotzen and by the end of the month were knocking on the door of Konigsberg.

Back in the southern section of the line the Germans were broken. The Russians advanced ninety miles in three days. Warsaw fell on 17 January and by the first week of February Marshal Zhukov's tanks had reached

Frankfurt on the Oder and were just fifty miles from Hitler's bunker in Berlin. Once inside German territory, the Red Army launched another vicious attack – this time on the civilian population. In a terrible act of retribution hundreds of villages were destroyed, their occupants often rounded up and murdered in cold blood. Thousands of German women were raped.

In a last ditch attempt to save the situation Hitler reorganised his military leadership, but instead of appointing an experienced military general to head up the crisis and take over the newly designated Army Group Vistula he appointed his *Reichsfuhrer SS* Heinrich Himmler, who, let's be honest, wasn't renowned for his strategic military competence. As if to hammer home this point, Himmler proceeded to appoint his commanders on their ability to tow the party line, rather than their ability to actually do the job. The Wehrmacht was fast becoming a farce.

Hell on Earth: Iwo Jima, 1945

After liberating the Philippines, American forces pushed on towards Japan. The next leap across the central Pacific Ocean was aimed at a tiny piece of volcanic rock just five miles long: Iwo Jima.

The island of Iwo Jima lay just 660 miles south of Tokyo and taking it would give the US air force a base from which they could raid almost any Japanese city at will. It was the most tantalising of objectives. The Japanese knew that the Americans would have their eye on this particular piece of rock and throughout the autumn and winter of 1944 they substantially strengthened the garrison there and constructed complex networks of underground tunnels and bunkers. The island commander was a Lieutenant General Tadamichi Kuribayashi and by the time the Americans waded up the beaches he had 22,000 men dug into well-prepared defensive positions along the interior of the island. The Japanese defensive plan on Iwo Jima was the same as on previous occasions – let the enemy land, draw them inland nice and easy and then grind them down in a brutal war of attrition.

Kuribayashi planned to make Iwo Jima Hell on earth.

However, it was the Americans who took the initiative in the 'make Iwo Jima a nasty place to be' stakes with an eye-watering aerial bombardment that lasted for more than seventy days – it was the longest sustained aerial offensive of the war – US naval guns also joined in the fun for a few days before the landings were due in an effort to knock out defensive strongholds. Iwo Jima was being smashed to pieces, yet all of this firepower did little to dent the fighting morale of the Japanese defenders, the majority of whom were hidden deep underground.

On the morning of 19 February 1945 the first waves of US Marines from the 4th and 5th Marine Divisions approached the shoreline, protected by a naval rolling barrage. Thick volcanic ash replaced the more familiar sandy beach and the shoreline was steep – add into the mix concentrated artillery fire from Japanese defensive positions cut into Mount Suribachi and you get some kind of idea of the welcome party that greeted those first waves of US Marines as they attempted to get ashore. The landing zones quickly became killing fields. Yet again the preliminary bombardment had failed to knock out enemy defenses. They would have to be eliminated one at a time by the men on the ground, just as soon as they managed to get off those beaches.

Over 500 Marines were killed on the first day of the offensive, yet somehow the initial waves of men managed to set up a bridgehead that quickly grew to almost 30,000 men. As the first tentative moves were made inland most of Kuribayashi's force remained hidden in their deep bunkers. Watching. Waiting for the right time to give the Americans an Imperial kick up the backside and chuck them back in the Pacific.

Just as Kuribayashi had hoped, the fighting quickly descended into a deadly game of attrition. Day after day the Marines inched forward, struggling against an enemy that seemingly favoured death to surrender. The Imperial commanders were waiting for the moment the Americans got fed up of their losses and turned around to head back home. But that moment never came. On 23 February, after several days of intense fighting, the American flag was raised on the summit of Mount Suribachi and one of the most iconic images of the war was born.

The actual photograph of the raising of the flag was in fact a stage replay of the first flag raising, which was carried out by E Company of the 28th Marine Corps who seized the summit even though parts of the mountain were still held by enemy units. The original flag was small and attached to a piece of piping. Later that day a second unit arrived on the scene with a larger flag and war photographer Joe Rosenthal brilliantly captured the moment of the men raising the second flag. The image was quickly wired to press agencies around the world and it became one of the most recognisable and iconic images of the whole war.

Meanwhile, on a particularly nasty hill nicknamed the 'Meat Grinder' the Marines were not in the mood for photographs. They were fighting for every yard of volcanic rock against fanatical defenders that were happy to die for their cause. Each defensive position, each tiny foxhole, each deep underground cave had to be individually captured using explosives and flamethrowers to flush out the enemy soldiers hiding within. It was a brutal fight to the death each and every time; very few prisoners were taken. Casualties were heavy on both sides.

Slowly the sheer weight of American firepower – from the land, sea and air – began to tell. The island's airfields were captured after a three-day struggle and eventually the Japanese were forced to retreat to the north of the island where they made their final stand at Kitano Point. It took ten days to clear that particular area and even when all hope was lost the Japanese launched a final, suicidal banzai charge. By 10 March organised resistance on Iwo Jima had all but ceased to exist, although each isolated defensive position continued to fight on independently. Sporadic fighting continued on the island into June; the Japanese were quite literally fighting until the last man.

The battle for Iwo Jima was over. It had taken over a month and had cost the lives of almost 6,000 Marines, with another 17,000 wounded. Of the 22,000 Japanese soldiers that were garrisoned on the island only 216 were taken alive.

The island's airstrips were immediately utilised, securing a safe air route to the Japanese home islands, no doubt saving the lives of thousands of aircrew. Now Iwo Jima had been captured and secured it was time to move in on Japan itself. Situated some 350 miles away from the Japanese mainland was the final barrier that stood in the way of a full-on Allied invasion of Japan:

The island of Okinawa.

Operation *Iceberg*: Okinawa, 1945

While the final acts of fighting were being played out on Iwo Jima plans were afoot for a massive invasion of Okinawa – the largest of the Ryukyu Islands situated just a few hundred miles away from the Japanese mainland.

Okinawa was a much larger island than Iwo Jima – sixty miles long and eighteen miles across at its widest point. Under the codename *Iceberg* preparations for the invasion of Okinawa were equal in scale to those of D-Day the previous year. Half a million men had been earmarked for the attack, backed up by over 1,200 naval vessels. Facing them would be 100,000 Imperial soldiers (not the 65,000 that US intelligence had indicated) under the stewardship of Lieutenant General Ushijima.

Deep down Ushijima knew he had little chance of victory. His plan was to hold out for as long as possible and inflict as many casualties on the Americans as he could. Just as on Iwo Jima, he positioned his men inland, organising strong defensive posts mainly in the hilly southern region. The Japanese also hoped to cause havoc out at sea as the Americans prepared for the invasion by utilising a number of very special weapons, namely Kamikazes.

The attack took place on 1 April 1945. A massive naval bombardment preceded the invasion while in the skies above the warships swarms of Kamikaze pilots dived straight towards their American targets. It was absolute chaos as hundreds of US Navy ships were attacked simultaneously by thousands of Kamikazes. Over thirty American warships were lost and another 200 were damaged. It is estimated that around 2,000 Kamikaze pilots successfully carried out their duty that morning.

The attacks were so ferocious and American casualties were so severe that at one point it seemed that the invasion might not take place at all.

However, the invasion did go ahead and the initial landings, carried out on the west coast of Okinawa, took place with little incident. Almost immediately the decision was made to carry on inland to seize vital airfields, these too were taken without incident. Twenty-four hours after the first landings the US forces had reached the east coast, effectively splitting the island in two. Marine units moved north quickly, encountering minimal opposition. By 15 April they had reached the very top of the island and five days later the whole northern section had been secured.

In the south it was not so easy.

The steep hills and narrow ravines in the south of the island provided the perfect defensive backdrop for the Japanese soldiers. The US 7th and 96th Infantry Divisions had been given the pleasure of clearing the southern area of the island; they hit stubborn resistance as early as 5 April but were still able to advance, albeit slowly. By 9 April Japanese resistance was so fierce it stopped the Americans in their tracks before a heavily defended strongpoint on Kakazu Ridge. For days the US forces launched repeated attacks on the ridge, but every time they were driven back. Despite being outnumbered almost two-to-one, the Japanese were defending their positions like men possessed. In four days of fighting on Kakazu Ridge the Japanese lost the thick end of 5,500 men killed in action. 451 Americans were killed.

On 4 May, in monsoon conditions that turned the ground to liquid mud, the Japanese launched a desperate counterattack that attempted to split the US Tenth Army in half. Despite brutal hand-to-hand combat the counterattack failed. It was then the Americans' turn to attack as they tried to put the boot in on the Japanese before they had time dust themselves down and regroup. This time the counterattack worked. Just. By the third week in May several key positions had changed hands and the Japanese forces were in danger of being completely surrounded, but before the Americans could move in for the kill the rains came again and quite literally washed out the attack.

General Ushijima took the opportunity to move his line to the extreme south of the island where they prepared to make their last stand. When the Americans reached the new positions they had to use napalm, explosives, flamethrowers and grenades to clear their enemy out of every foxhole, every machine-gun post, every pillbox and every bunker they came across. Each position, no matter how small, took huge efforts to clear. Most of the time the defenders only stopped fighting when they were dead. By 17 June the defenders were squeezed into a small parcel of land only eight miles square, but they carried on fighting and repeatedly refused requests to surrender and end the slaughter. Finally, on 21 June Japanese resistance ended. That same day General Ushijima committed *hara-kiri* (suicide). As on Iwo Jima, pockets of resistance continued to cause mayhem up until 2 July, when Okinawa was finally declared secure.

The largest land battle of the Pacific War was finally over.

More than 49,000 American soldiers had been killed or wounded, USAAF had lost over 750 planes and the US Navy had lost thirty-six ships and had over 350 vessels damaged. But these losses were nothing compared to those of the Imperial Japanese Armed Forces. Out of the 100,000 men that started the fight, only 7,400 were left alive. Thousands of Kamikaze pilots had been lost and the Imperial Japanese Navy had lost sixteen ships including the giant *Yamato* battleship.

The path to Japan was finally free and open, but the insane loss of life incurred while capturing the tiny islands of Okinawa and Iwo Jima meant that the American top brass were considering unleashing an ultra secret weapon on Japan in a desperate effort to limit the number of American casualties.

Enter the atomic bomb.

From the *Westwall* to the Elbe, 1945

Whichever way you looked at it, the Germans had found themselves on the end of a severe beating in the Ardennes and they began 1945 physically, psychologically and logistically broken. The German generals in the field were desperate to retreat back to the east bank of the Rhine and regroup, but Hitler wasn't in the mood for any kind of retreat. In his eyes, retreat was an admission of failure and he simply would not sanction it. No. His army would stand and fight on the west bank of the Rhine.

On the other side of the wire the Allies were dusting themselves down and getting ready for the final advance into Germany. Eisenhower favoured an approach along a broad front – à la the Red Army in the East – and by early January he had over seventy divisions at his disposal, many of which were armoured, as well as an overwhelming show of air power. In his eyes the Nazis didn't stand a chance.

The Allied plan was made up of three phases: phase one –kick the Wehrmacht off of the west bank of the Rhine; phase two – initiate several river crossings up and down the Rhine and get across to the east side; phase three – a broad general advance made up of two simultaneous moves. Field Marshal Montgomery's 21st Army Group would take the bulk of the available men and skirt north of the industrial Ruhr region and occupy northern Germany, meanwhile General Bradley's 12th Army Group would push south of the Ruhr (technically encircling this vital region) heading towards the River Elbe before crossing into Austria and Czechoslovakia where they planned to meet up with the Russians.

Not everyone liked the plan. Montgomery would have preferred a narrower front, allowing him make a bee line for Berlin. Bradley hated the fact he was playing second fiddle to Montgomery. The British top brass didn't think Eisenhower had enough resources to mount two attacks at the same time.

Eisenhower ignored them all. The attack was pencilled in for 8 February.

Preparations continued all through January. By the beginning of February the Allied armies were lined up and ready to advance along Germany's borders with Holland, Belgium, Luxembourg and France. Although several forays through the *Westwall* (also known as the Siegfried Line) had already taken place, the only time it had been permanently breached was at Aachen.

That was all about to change. The stage was set for the final push into Germany.

Before dawn on 8 February 1,400 big guns of the Canadian First Army barked into life throughout the northern part of the line, smashing down on the very surprised units of the German 84th Division. No one wearing the Nazi eagle thought that Montgomery would even dare to contemplate attacking in this sector. It would mean advancing through marshy ground with flooded plains on one side and the Reichswald Forest on the other and that would be madness. Wouldn't it?

Not in the eyes of Montgomery. At 10:30hrs he blew the bugle to begin the infantry advance on the unsuspecting enemy. On a narrow seven-mile front from the River Maas to the River Waal on the Dutch/German border the XXX Corps of Lieutenant General Horrocks attacked. By the end of the day the Germans had lost over 1,000 men and were on the run. This was all a bit too easy.

Success like that couldn't last and it didn't. The Germans quickly dusted themselves down, reorganised and moved extra panzer divisions up from the south into the fight. The battle that ensued – owing to thick mud, pounding rain and deliberate flooding – quickly started to resemble the First World War battle of Passchendaele. The Allied advance in the north was reduced to a crawl but it also weakened German resistance in the south substantially. Consequently, when the US Ninth Army to the south moved forward on 23 February they had a much easier time of things despite a mad scramble by the Germans to send some *panzers* back south again. By 10 March the Germans had incurred over 50,000 casualties in this sector and had been forced back beyond the Rhine.

Further south Bradley's US Twelfth Army Group smashed their way rapidly through the *Westwall* (which was much more lightly defended in their sector) and by 6 March they had entered Cologne. In order to keep up the pressure on the retreating enemy a detachment was sent off to try and capture the city of Bonn. It was during this advance that Brigadier General Hoge, commanding Combat Group B of the US 9th Armored Division heard the news that there was a bridge still intact across the Rhine at Remagen. It was an opportunity too good to miss.

Blatantly ignoring his orders he raced to Remagen and at 16:00hrs he was at the Ludendorff bridge. The Germans had planted explosives all along the bridge but for some reason the charges wouldn't detonate. US Lieutenant John Battenfield went onto the Ludendorff bridge, found the explosive charges and disconnected the detonators.

Twenty-four hours after crossing the bridge 8,000 troops were brought in to defend the bridgehead. To Bradley's immense satisfaction, the Americans were across the Rhine.

Upon hearing the news Hitler flew into a rage of apocalyptic proportions. Not only did he have the commanding officer of the defending unit shot, but he also shot a number of other soldiers that had no direct involvement with the failure of the detonation. He also went into overdrive in an effort to destroy both the bridge and the Americans who had captured it. He ordered immediate air strikes, he sent in the 11th Panzer Division from Bonn, he ordered his artillery to smash the area and he even ordered a V-2 rocket strike to be launched against the bridge. Finally on 17 March, the bridge collapsed, by this time the Americans had not only built another bridge across the river but had managed to deploy four more divisions, including one armoured division, on the eastern side of the Rhine.

Wunderbar!

Not quite so *wunderbar* for General Bradley was the fact that he was not allowed to exploit this victory as it did not fit in with Eisenhower's tactical plan which favoured a massed crossing in the north (opposite the town of Wesel) by Montgomery on 24 March. Bradley had to be content with sweeping the eastern bank of the Rhine to cut off any potential enemy reinforcements. Montgomery may have lost the race to the Rhine, but he was not too far behind and when he did cross, he did it in style.

On the night of 23 March, Montgomery started the operation to move his men across the Rhine. Twenty-four divisions would cross along a thirty-five mile stretch of river. The date of the crossing had been delayed in order to stockpile enough supplies of materials, ammunition and fuel to get them through what they expected to be an intense firefight on the other side of the Rhine. What Montgomery didn't know was that opposite him were just five German divisions as Hitler had decided to move the bulk of his Western defenders to the East to help stave off the Russians as he thought the Allies had exhausted themselves from their recent exertions.

Not for the first time, Hitler was sadly mistaken.

The crossing was preceded by a huge aerial and artillery bombardment of key defensive positions and strongpoints. Over three days RAF Bomber Command and their friends in the USAAF flew over 16,000 sorties dropping almost 50,000 tonnes of explosives. A staggering 60,000 infantry crossed the river in amphibious tanks and landing craft, under cover of a huge smokescreen that was laid across the entire length of the attack front. The men on the river were backed up by two airborne divisions who dropped over 16,000 paras in behind enemy lines to occupy the enemy and silence any enemy artillery positions still standing after the bombing. There were also over 50,000 engineers on site to build enough bridges to get another million men across over the coming days and weeks. It was an impressive show of strength.

Casualties were light and in no time a bridgehead was set up on the east side of the Rhine and the engineers got busy building bridges to enable the rest of the men and materials to get across the river quickly. Meanwhile British Commandos were already inside the town of Wesel clearing out German defenders. Winston Churchill watched the assault unfold from a command post on the western side of the river.

By 26 March the engineers had built seven bridges and they were all open to traffic streaming across from the west. Meanwhile the infantry advanced east along both sides of the Lippe – a tributary of the Rhine. Although the final result was perhaps a foregone conclusion, pockets of German resistance fought with a fanatical determination and skill, it was not always a straightforward fight. That said, the sheer power and scale of the Allied armies overwhelmed even the most ardent of defenders and by 1 April Field Marshal Model and the entire *Wehrmacht* Army Group B were being backed into a corner in the Ruhr region as Allied troops that had crossed the Rhine in the north and south fanned out and closed in. Three weeks later over 300,000 men of Army Group B surrendered and Field Marshal Model committed suicide.

Meanwhile the advance continued apace, during April on the Western Front almost 50,000 German prisoners were being taken every single day. In the north sections of Montgomery's 21st Army Group had reached the north Baltic coast. Further south the US Ninth Army had reached the River Elbe at Magdeburg on 12 April. On 25 April the US First Army reached the River Elbe at Torgau where they met up with units of the Russian First Ukrainian Army Group. They were within sniffing distance of Berlin. It was just a matter of time before Germany was utterly defeated.

As the Allied juggernaut steamrollered through the Greater German Reich they started to uncover clear evidence of something so terrible, so sinister, so inhumane it would send shockwaves through the world.

Holocaust: Liberating the Camps, 1945

Soviet forces were the first to see at first-hand what kind of treatment the Germans had been dishing out to so-called *untermensch* (literally translated as 'under men' or inferior people). On 22 July 1944 they reached the Majdanek camp near Lublin, Poland. By the time they got there the Nazis had already moved on, leaving behind them around 1,000 emaciated prisoners. In an attempt to hide any evidence the Germans had demolished the camp and set fire to the large crematorium used to burn bodies. In their haste the gas chambers were left intact as were a few buildings containing hair, suitcases, clothing and children's toys.

After Majdanek, the Red Army also discovered the sites of the Belzec, Sobibor and Treblinka death camps, but as most of the Polish Jews had already been dealt with, all of these camps had been fully dismantled in 1943. As the Red Army continued their sweep through Poland they entered a small town about thirty miles to the west of Krakow called Oświęcim.

It was an unassuming town in most respects, yet it housed the largest human killing factory ever built. The Soviets walked through the gates of Auschwitz on 27 January 1945 but found it largely deserted. In November 1944 Himmler had ordered the gassing of prisoners to stop and Crematoria II, III and IV were dismantled, while Crematorium I was transformed into an air raid shelter. Written documents were burnt, as were many of the camp buildings in an effort to destroy evidence. On 17 January 1945 58,000 Auschwitz inmates were evacuated under guard and force-marched to the East in an effort to hide them from the Allies. Only a few thousand of the weakest inmates were left behind, many were on the verge of death. Although much of the camp had been destroyed, the Russians still found stores containing hundreds of thousands of men's suits, women's coats and dresses and over seven tonnes of human hair. Further interrogation of Russian inmates revealed the true horrors of what had been going on beyond the gates of Auschwitz.

It is surprising now, but at the time the camp's liberation received little press attention, maybe because they had already discovered a similar camp at Majdanek. They had allowed some members of the press into Majdanek, but no one was allowed near Auschwitz until after the German surrender in May.

No extermination camps were built in the West, instead the US and British forces came across Nazi concentration camps. On 11 April men from the US 6th Armored Division liberated more than 20,000 prisoners in the Buchenwald concentration camp near Weimar. A few days later on 15 April the British VIII Corps entered a large camp at Bergen-Belsen.

In December 1944 Bergen-Belsen was 'home' to around 15,000 prisoners, but by April 1945, courtesy of numerous death marches and transportations from the death camps further east, this number had grown to between 50–60,000. The camp housed thousands of unburied bodies and was infested with Typhus; disease was rampant throughout the camp. There was virtually no food or clean water for the inmates and even after liberation they continued to drop like flies, in fact more than 10,000 died in the weeks after liberation. Camp guards and the local civilian population were forced to help with clearing the bodies and burying the dead, a scene that was repeated often in camps throughout Germany. Bergen-Belsen was burnt down in June 1945 but to this day the site remains a memorial site to those killed or affected by the Holocaust.

On 29 April a unit of the US 45th Division unlocked the gates at Dachau, as they approached the camp they passed thirty-nine railway carts full to the brim with dead and decomposing bodies. SS guards tried to open fire on the would-be liberators but were rushed by prisoners and beaten to death in the ultimate taste of their own medicine. There were approximately 70,000 prisoners still alive at Dachau.

The men unlocking the gates of these camps witnessed unspeakable conditions and scenarios; as well as the thousands of corpses that lay unburied, there were mass graves full of thousands more; there were warehouses full of belongings, human hair and gold teeth that had been extracted from the bodies. There was clear evidence of cruel medical experiments, of torture, of malnutrition and forced labour. Many men flew into rages at what they had seen, many more would suffer psychologically as they carried the visions of those camps with them for years and years to come.

The small percentage of inmates who survived resembled nothing more than living skeletons. Many were so weak that they could hardly move. Disease remained an ever-present danger, and many of the camps had to be burned down to prevent the spread of epidemics. Survivors of the camps faced a long and difficult road to recovery, some even felt guilty that they had survived when so many of their friends and family had been killed.

Finale in the West: Berlin, 1945

In the wake of the Battle of the Bulge, Hitler felt compelled to issue *The Basic Order for the Preparations to Defend the Capital* which went public on 9 March 1945. Deep down Hitler still didn't think the Allies had the resources to reach Berlin and had issued the order more to inspire the people of Berlin and to show his enemies that Germany was prepared to defend her capital 'to the last person and to the last cartridge'.

By mid-April the US First and Ninth Armies were camped on the banks of the Elbe. In fact sections of the US Ninth Army had built a bridgehead at Magdeburg and were straining at the leash, desperate to be allowed to head on to Berlin, just seventy miles away.

Eisenhower said no.

On 28 March Eisenhower had sent a telegram to Stalin to reassure him that he did not intend to make a run for Berlin. He would leave the city for the Russians. Churchill and the British government thought he was mad to simply let the Russians capture Berlin, but Eisenhower was under increasing pressure to end the war as quickly as possible and the Russians were already much closer to Berlin and had millions of men chomping at the bit. The simple fact was that the Red Army had the best chance of taking the city. Eisenhower had the full backing of the US Chiefs of Staff – his decision was final.

Ironically, Stalin didn't believe him and used this message as a signal to press the put their foot down and get into Berlin before those pesky Westerners. Slowly but surely German strongpoints and fortresses were silenced and by the beginning of April approximately 2 million men, across twenty separate army groups were in position, ably supported by over 3,000 tanks and 7,500 aircraft.

The Russian army groups were dispersed across three fronts that formed a wide semi-circle within spitting distance of their target. In the south was

Marshal Konev's 1st Ukrainian Front with seven armies. He was to advance towards the Elbe and move up to Berlin if the others needed him. Marshal Zhukov was in the centre with his 1st Belorussian Front, he had ten armies and was situated exactly opposite the German Ninth Army. Zhukov's one and only task was to encircle and capture Berlin. To the north of Zhukov was the 2nd Belorussian Front led by Marshal Rokossovsky – his task was to clear German resistance and ensure Zhukov's flank was secure.

From a German point of view, what was left of Army Group Centre held decent defensive positions along the Seelow Heights, some fifty-six miles to the east of Berlin, as well as heavily fortified positions in and around the city. Army Group Centre had a paper strength of around 1 million men but many of these were members of the *Volkssturm* (Hitler's People's Army made up of teenagers and old men who were not in active service elsewhere.) They only had about 1,500 tanks and just a handful of planes. Berlin itself was quickly fortified after the defeat in the Ardennes with the construction of barricades, strongpoints and large water ditches throughout the city.

On 16 April 1945, the seventy-fifth anniversary of Lenin's birth, the massed ranks of the Russian artillery on the east side of Germany burst into life. In the centre of the front, opposite Berlin, there were 400 guns per mile. During the course of the fight for the capital these guns would hurl over 1.8 million shells onto the city – more than one for every resident.

As the artillery smashed the German defensive positions Zhukov launched his attack. Stalin wanted the job done quickly in case the Americans got to Berlin first and as such Zhukov had planned to conquer the Seelow Heights on day one of the offensive. However Zhukov didn't account for such fierce German resistance, the Russians barely made any progress on the first day against well-positioned and motivated defenders. It took two full days before the Seelow Heights were in Russian hands and it cost Zhukov 30,000 men.

Zhukov's problems didn't stop there. Once he had clambered over the Seelow Heights, his men wandered straight into a further defensive zone lying just beyond. Despite having overwhelming numbers of men at his disposal, Zhukov was having a bit of a nightmare.

Not so for Konev in the south, there the Russians were making great progress and he was subsequently given permission by Stalin to turn his armies north towards Berlin, thus signalling the start of a race between him and Zhukov as to who would capture the city first.

By 20 April (Hitler's fifty-sixth birthday) Zhukov had regained his momentum and forward detachments of his Eighth Guards Army reached the eastern suburbs of Berlin and began the shelling of the central city areas. To the north German resistance finally crumbled and Zhukov's armies were well on the way to completing a full encirclement. It still wasn't an easy gig though. The closer the Red Army got to the centre of Berlin, the stronger the German defense was, bolstered by artillery, tanks and *Panzerfausts* (anti-tank weapons). This slowdown in the advance gave the Russian soldiers, many of whom were very poor back home, the opportunity to help themselves to some of the local delicacies. In April 1945 the number of parcels being sent back home to the Soviet Union from soldiers in the Reich had increased by 1,000 times since January of the same year. Huge amounts of food were being sent home to families as well as books, paintings, clothes, shoes, bedding and radios.

Konev continued to move north to link up with Zhukov, which he did on 22 April. By 24 April Berlin was totally surrounded.

By now Hitler was personally in charge of the defence of Berlin. He was also even more delusional than normal. He had dispatched Field Marshal Keitel and Colonel General Jodl to command the counter-attacks that were (in his mind) going to totally annihilate the Soviet invaders. Meanwhile he and Goebbels were going to rally the 90,000 boys and grandpas of the *Volkssturm* and hold off the might of the Red Army indefinitely.

#asmadasaboxoffrogs

On 26 April Zhukov and Konev launched an attack on the Propaganda Ministry building and the following day they took control of the Postdamer Strasse Bridge. The fighting was brutal; many Berliners were taking their Führer's order to fight to the last man and last cartridge very literally indeed. On 30 April several more government buildings were taken and Zhukov launched three separate assaults on the Reichstag. Each one failed but eventually they were able to eventually clear a path for their tanks to get close to the building. At about 14:30hrs rumours were rife that a Soviet flag had been seen fluttering over the Reichstag and, thinking that the rumours were true, Zhukov sent a triumphant message back to headquarters. Later it became clear that no flag had flown, which was a problem. If Stalin ever found out about his little 'mistake' he would be in a whole world of trouble.

For Zhukov, the most important thing in the whole world was to get a flag flying on top of the Reichstag. Fast.

It took another ten hours of hand-to-hand fighting within the corridors of the Reichstag before a group of Russians found their way up a back staircase and managed to secure a flag around a statue on the roof. The flag that flew from the burning building that night was no ordinary flag. It was the banner of victory. Two days later, the remnants of the German Berlin garrison surrendered.

The battle for Berlin cost the Red Army around 100,000 men. Zhukov commented afterwards that for him it was one of the most difficult battles of the war. But if it was difficult for him and his Red Army, it was hellish for the boys and old men that were tasked to defend their capital alongside the remnants of the Wehrmacht.

Total German losses are unknown.

Suicides and Surrender: Victory in Europe, 1945

In Italy the fighting was going exactly the same way as in Germany. The US Fifth Army, along with the British Eighth Army, launched a new initiative on 9 April to kick the Axis out of Italy for good. The Americans were to attack Bologna and then swing out to the west, while the British would move up the east coast towards Treviso and round to Trieste.

Waves of bombers smashed seven bells out of the German positions in preparation for the infantry advances and although the men were slightly delayed due to bad weather, they didn't hang about once they got going. The US Fifth Army reached the outskirts of Bologna by 20 April and was in control of Verona just six days later. A segment then swung west towards Milan. Meanwhile the British Eighth Army also moved rapidly north, facing very little serious opposition, and liberated Venice on 29 April before moving on to Trieste. By now garrisons were surrendering left right and centre – it was just a matter of time before the complete collapse of the Italian Front.

Meanwhile Mussolini, still nominal head of the Italian Social Republic, and his mistress Clara Petacci were trying to escape to Switzerland, but they were spotted, captured and executed. Their bodies were taken to Milan and hung upside down in the Piazzale Loreto for the world to see.

Back in Berlin, Hitler was holed up in his underground bunker contemplating how it had all gone so spectacularly wrong. In six years his Nazi regime had gone from the undisputed champions of Europe to total disaster resulting in the destruction of his adopted Fatherland. Ironically it was the 'inferior Russians' that were delivering the final blow to his Aryan dream and he was adamant that he would not be taken alive by those barbarians. Especially after what happened to Mussolini recently. No, for the Führer, there would be only one way out of this mess.

On 30 April 1945, having tested an arsenic pill on his dog Blondi the day before, Hitler and his new wife Eva Braun retired to a small room in his underground bunker. Braun took her own life with poison while Hitler shot himself in the head. Their bodies were taken out to the garden of the Chancellery and burned before the Russians could get their hands on them. Many others who had spent the last few weeks of the war with Hitler chose a similar fate. On 1 May, Joseph Goebbels and his wife Magda poisoned their six young children before committing suicide themselves.

Before he pulled the trigger Hitler wrote his political testament in which he named Grand Admiral Karl Doenitz as his successor and Reich President. Based up in Flensburg the first thing Doenitz did was to organise the surrender of the Axis forces.

The first surrender came in Italy where a ceasefire negotiated on 29 April came into effect on 2 May. On 4 May German forces in northern Germany and the Netherlands surrendered to Field Marshal Montgomery and on 4 May German forces in Bavaria also waved the white flag. That same day Doenitz ordered Hitler's wartime Chief of Operations, General Alfred Jodl, to travel to the French city of Rheims and surrender to the Western Allies.

At 02:40hrs in the early morning of 7 May 1945 a short ceremony took place in a schoolhouse in Rheims. Under the watchful gaze of assorted Allied officers and seventeen invited journalists, Jodl signed the act of surrender. After he had signed Jodl addressed the room:

'I want to say a word. With this signature the German people and the German armed forces are for better or worse delivered into the victor's hands. In this war, which has lasted more than five years, they both have achieved and suffered more than perhaps any other people in the world. In this hour I can only express the hope that the victor will treat them with generosity.'

After this, the German delegation left in silence. After they left a message was sent to the War Office in London:

'The mission of this Allied Force was fulfilled at 02.41, local time, May 7th, 1945'

Those Allied officers that had witnessed the signing celebrated by drinking champagne out of mess tins.

Stalin wasn't in the mood for champagne. He refused to accept the Rheims documents and accused the Americans and British of putting together a 'shady deal' with Germany. He thought the enemy should be forced to sign a surrender document to the occupiers of Berlin and that the proceedings should be centred round a Soviet general, not an American. A second surrender document was prepared in Moscow which was signed by Field Marshal Keitel for Germany, Marshal Zhukov for the Soviet Union, Air Chief Marshal Arthur Tedder for the British Empire, General Carl Spaatz for the USA and General de Lattre de Tassigny for France.

The war in Europe was finally over.

Little Boy and Fatman: The Destruction of Japan, 1945

It was bemusing to the Allies that, after the death of Hitler and the end of the war in Europe, the Japanese didn't take the hint and give up the fight gracefully. If anything they fought with more fanaticism than ever. The islands of Iwo Jima and Okinawa were only given up to the Americans after the defenders had quite literally fought to the death. In Burma Anglo-Indian forces led by General Slim had eventually won the day after a very dangerous nocturnal amphibious landing. Over 150,000 Japanese soldiers died in Burma – only 2,000 were taken prisoner. If this was the kind of defense they were going to put up on remote territories, what would they be like if the Americans dared to invade mainland Japan?

It was a thought that the Allied top brass didn't want to contemplate. They needed a plan to break Japan without the need for invasion. Enter USAAF Major General Curtis LeMay.

American B-29 bombers had been bombing the Japan mainland sporadically since October 1944 but their journeys were long and dangerous and their accuracy was nothing to shout about. LeMay was brought in to change all that and bomb Japan into submission.

He ordered his B-29s to be stripped of much of their armour and guns to increase their effective range and carrying capacity. He also fundamentally changed tactics. Low-level bombing of Japanese cities with high explosives, incendiary bombs and napalm would now be the order of the day. Actually, it would be the order of the night, because LeMay wanted to give the inhabitants of Japan a nice bedtime surprise and hit them at night. After a few small tests the first full-scale night attack on Japan was scheduled in for 9/10 March.

The target was Tokyo.

That night the bombers of the US 21st Bomber Command dropped about 2,000 tonnes of bombs onto Tokyo. At that time, Tokyo, like many

Japanese cities, was largely comprised of thousands of wooden buildings tightly packed together, not surprisingly the result of the bombing was devastating. A huge firestorm quickly developed that was visible to the aircrews for almost 150 miles. Sixteen square miles of the city was completely wiped off of the map, an eye-watering 1 million people were made homeless and over 124,000 people were killed or injured. As well as the massive civilian destruction, the raid also obliterated many crucial industrial plants that supplied the Imperial war effort. In return for all of this damage the USAAF lost just fourteen bombers and forty-two crew members.

LeMay was delighted, and rightly so. It looked like he might have found the key to kicking Japan out of the war for good. Another raid, this time on Nagoya, the centre of Japanese aircraft manufacturing, was quickly planned for the night of 18/19 March.

However, the results of this second massive raid (almost 300 B-29s were involved) were not as devastating as LeMay was hoping for. More bombs were dropped on Nagoya than were dropped on Tokyo, but there was no firestorm, no mass destruction of industrial buildings and no general civilian disaster. Not to be deterred, the bombers were back in the air within forty-eight hours, this time they had the ship-building city of Osaka in their bombsights. Again over 300 B-29s flocked to the city and smashed it to pieces with over 1,700 tonnes of explosives. Another devastating firestorm engulfed part of the city, but this time the civilian population were better prepared and casualties were much lighter than in Tokyo – 'only' 4,000 died with another 8,000 injured. Over eight square miles of the city were erased, 135,000 houses and 119 major production facilities were burnt out.

Throughout March and April the raids kept coming and as the campaign moved into May the frequency and intensity of the raids actually increased as LeMay managed to get his hands on more resources from Southeast Asia. On the night of 23/24 May Tokyo was visited by 562 B-29s – the largest single B-29 raid of the war – the results were predictable:

another huge firestorm and the city reduced by about five square miles. The bombers returned to Tokyo forty-eight hours later with what turned out to be the most destructive non-nuclear raid of the whole war. A staggering 16.8 square miles of the city was destroyed with many key government buildings (including parts of the Imperial Palace) succumbing to the flames.

After these two monumental beatings, literally half of Tokyo had been destroyed. Finally it was taken off of the USAAF target list.

Other cities were not so lucky. By the end of June over a hundred square miles of Japan's largest cities were totally destroyed, but even that wasn't the end of it – punishment was dished out almost daily throughout the summer but despite all of this; despite the general situation being totally hopeless; despite the civilian population being on the brink of starvation; despite disease running rife; despite industry output being practically nonexistent and despite the threat of invasion a nailed-on certainty, Japan still did not surrender.

On 26 July Allied leaders warned Japan to surrender 'immediately and unconditionally' or suffer the pain of 'utter destruction'. Two days later the Japanese High Command responded to the warning – they would carry on the fight.

The Allies had a choice to make – the naval blockade that had been in place around Japan for some months would, given time, force the enemy to surrender but many army leaders wanted to send out a stronger message, not only to Japan, but to Russia as well.

It was time to introduce the world to a new kind of weapon. The most terrible weapon man had yet devised.

After waiting a few days for clear weather, the morning of 6 August dawned bright and clear. Colonel Paul W. Tibbets climbed aboard his B-29 *Enola Gay* (named after his Mum) and headed out to the Japanese city of

Hiroshima. On board the Enola Gay that morning was a very special passenger; a 9,000lb nuclear bomb known affectionately as 'Little Boy'. The three aircraft that would deliver the bomb arrived over the city at 08:06hrs. They flew so high (31,000 feet) that many on the ground didn't give them a second thought. Eyewitnesses reported that the two aircraft either side of the lead bomber suddenly banked away very quickly just after a strange object with a parachute was dropped.

The town of Hiroshima was chosen as the primary target for 'Little Boy' since it had remained largely untouched by conventional bombing raids, therefore the bomb's effects could be clearly measured. Hiroshima was also a major port and a military headquarters, and as such a valid target for action.

At just after 08:15hrs the bomb detonated. The blast wave destroyed practically everything within a radius of five miles. In an instant 80,000 people were dead with many thousands more badly burnt and injured. Three-quarters of the city was reduced to rubble in a matter of seconds. A huge mushroom cloud of debris rose boiling into the atmosphere, higher than the aircraft that had delivered the devastation. Looking out of his window at the cloud, the *Enola Gay* co-pilot, Captain Robert Lewis, commented: 'My God, what have we done?'

If things weren't desperate enough for Japan, Stalin came good on a promise he had given to the other Allied leaders to help out with Japan three months after the end of the war in Europe. At midnight on 8 August the Japanese ambassador in Moscow received the Russian documentation of war. Before the ink had dried on the paperwork, a million Russian troops began the march towards Manchuria.

While the Red Army was on route another group of three B-29 bombers made their way to Nagasaki carrying another deadly payload. The second atomic bomb was known as 'Fat Man' and detonated at 11:02hrs just to the northwest of downtown Nagasaki. Of the 286,000 people living in Nagasaki at the time of the blast, 35,000 people were killed.

The devastation of these two atomic bombs, plus Russia declaring war and carving its way through Manchuria convinced Emperor Hirohito that the game was finally up for Japan. For the last ten years he had been nothing more than a puppet leader – it was the military leaders that had made the big decisions, but they had failed. After a meeting with his so called 'advisors' he decided to offer up Japan's surrender on one condition, that the sovereign power of the emperor would be retained. The message was sent to the Americans who replied swiftly; surrender was to be unconditional.

After a short period of deliberation, the emperor agreed to these terms. Radio messages were sent out to all Japanese troops telling them of the surrender and that they were to lay down their weapons. It was over. Most did as they were asked; some did not and fought on. Many officers committed suicide rather than suffering the humiliation of surrendering to the Americans.

On 2 September 1945 the newly appointed Foreign Minister of Japan, Mamoru Shigemitsu, signed the formal surrender documents on board the battleship USS *Missouri*. General Douglas MacArthur along with delegates from Britain, China, Russia, New Zealand, Canada, Australia, France and the Netherlands countersigned on behalf of the Allies.

The Second World War had finally ended.

Aftermath

In terms of lives lost the Second World War was the most deadly conflict in history. Getting a definitive number on actual body count is nigh on impossible and every book you read will give you a different number, but it is generally thought that military deaths are in the region of 20–25 million people with another 30 million civilian deaths as a result of direct military action such as bombings. For those of you who are not good at maths that is 50–55 million people. It is a number that I personally have trouble comprehending, I often try to imagine casualty numbers for battles in terms of 'numbers of full Wembley stadiums' but for the Second World War you end up with over 611 Wembley Stadiums full with the dead. If that isn't enough blood for you, you can always add in the number of people that were killed by war-related disease and famine, that's another 20–28 million souls. Enough to fill up another 311 Wembley stadiums.

Individually the biggest losers were the Soviet Union with about 27 million dead, China with between 15 and 20 million dead, Germany with around 7 million, Poland with around 6 million and Japan with around 3 million people dead.

All told, we are looking at the thick end of 80 million people dead. EIGHTY MILLION. It is a number that is just truly, truly staggering.

Cities all over the world had been reduced to rubble, this was particularly true in Germany which had suffered intense air attacks from the RAF and the USAAF; the Soviet Union which had suffered terribly during her fight with Nazi Germany; and Japan which had been smashed by the USAAF and had been on the wrong end of not one, but two atomic bombs.

The widespread destruction of homes, schools, offices, factories and hospitals meant that millions of people were on the move, looking for new places to live, ideally places that were not completely destroyed. Some took to the streets of their own accord such as those people who had been transported to Germany or Poland and forced to work in concentration camps. Others were forced to leave as many of the newly formed governments started to kick out various minority groups and political threats. The United Nations (set up in 1945 in the vain hope of trying to keep the peace) set up special camps for these Displaced Persons (DPs) and by 1947 over 7 million people called these DP camps home. Many of these people did find a new home though, as a number of countries faced a severe shortage of manpower after the war and actively encouraged immigration. Britain was among these countries that offered immediate resettlement for skilled workers and for qualified foreign nationals in an effort to bridge the post-war skills gap.

European political order was turned on its head during the post-war years with the Soviet Union achieving almost complete political dominance over Poland, Czechoslovakia, Rumania, Bulgaria, Hungary and the eastern sector of Germany by the end of 1948. Berlin, although physically deep inside the eastern sector of Germany that was run by the Russians, was split into British, Soviet, American and French sectors. Seeing the Soviet Union gain such influence in Europe worried the Western Allies greatly and relationships cooled quickly. The Americans and the other Western Allies were nervous about the potential for Communism to spread further West, especially when Europe's economy was still very weak. In an effort to negate this potential problem the USA announced the European Recovery Plan (otherwise known as the Marshall Plan) in June 1947. This plan offered economic aid to countries devastated by the war but nothing was offered to the Soviet Union or any country under its wing. This act annoyed Stalin greatly. In an effort to kick the Western Allies out of Berlin, Stalin initiated a blockade on the city from June 1948 to May 1949. During these months the civilian population of the three zones of western Berlin were fed and supplied by the very same air forces that had been smashing them to pieces just a few years before in what was known as the Berlin Airlift.

Despite British and American pleas for the Soviet Union to allow the nations of central and Eastern Europe to govern themselves, Stalin carried on with his own policy of ensuring domestic security. He saw these countries as a barrier between him and another invasion from the West – he wasn't about to give it up. He didn't trust those Westerners and they didn't trust him. Fear, suspicion and mis-trust dominated the political scene. To counter the threat of a Russian attack the western European nations along with the USA and Canada formed the North Atlantic Treaty Organisation (NATO) which guaranteed mutual assistance if it all got a bit steamy with the Red Army. Most importantly, this agreement meant that western Europe could now hide behind the nuclear protection of America.

Not to be outdone by NATO, the Soviet Union and its allies (including China, which had also become Communist under Mao Zedong) put together the Council for Mutual Economic Assistance (COMECON) in 1949. Europe was now divided into two armed camps but at the time of signing only NATO boasted atomic weapons with the USA. Within months the Russians successfully tested their own nuclear weapons – the Cold War was born.

In other parts of the world the immediate post-war years were just as chaotic. Intense internal pressure led to British India being granted independence and subsequently partitioned into India and Pakistan in 1947. A year later both Burma and Ceylon (Sri Lanka) also achieved independence. British colonial presence in South Asia had come to an end in the blink of an eye.

In Japan the civilian population had to quickly get used to the fact that not only had they lost a war with America, but also that an American-led administration was heading up Japanese reconstruction and rehabilitation. One of the first things General MacArthur decided was that those men who had led Japan to war would be tried as war criminals, he also made sweeping changes to Japan's constitution, including expanding the role of women in general society, the introduction of trade unions and land reforms.

In the Middle East the UN, in an effort to sort out the lingering problem that had existed since 1917 of finding a homeland for the Jewish people, split Palestine into two areas and moved 100,000 Jewish refugees in. On 14 May 1948 the Zionists declared the new state of Israel – the USA and the Soviet Union officially gave it thumbs up the very next day. The surrounding Arab states all declared war on Israel but were defeated and in the aftermath of that particular scrap Israel actually expanded its original borders. In doing so almost a million Palestinian Arabs were kicked out and forced to live as refugees. Even to this day the tension in this area is high.

As all of these separate confrontations show, the end of the Second World War did not ultimately bring about instant global harmony. Yes, Fascism had been defeated, but out of its ashes arose the spectre of Communism. German expansion had been replaced with Soviet expansion. Military aggression had been overcome, but with the result of splitting the world into two very large, very deadly military super groups.

It would be a very uneasy peace.

Maps

Here are a selection of maps that may help bring some of the narrative to life.

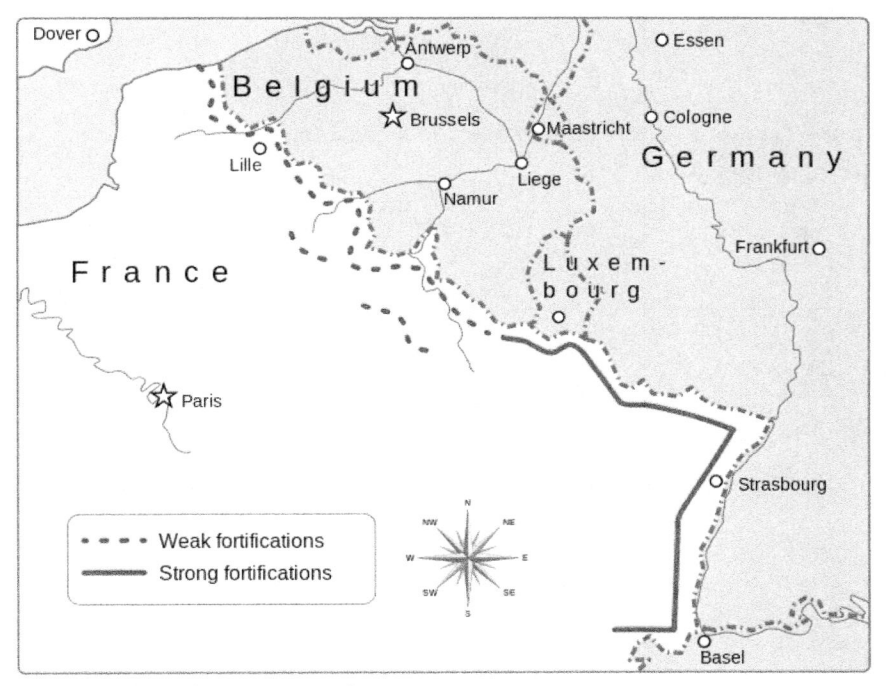

Map showing the Maginot Line.
Source: Goran tek-en (Wikepedia) Copyright free

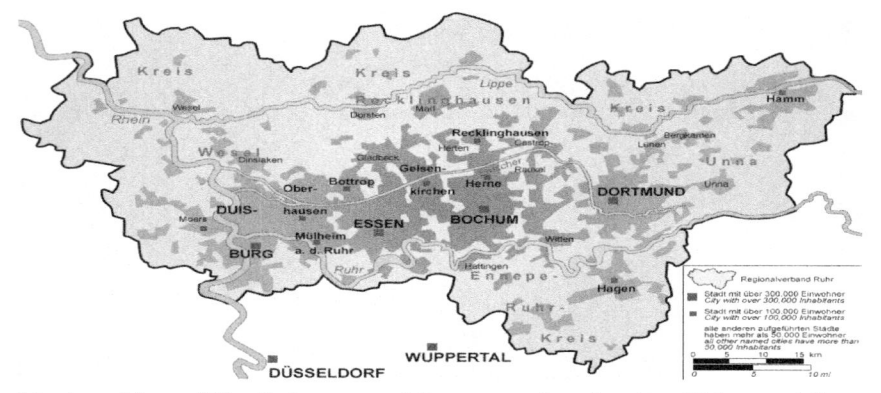

Modern Map of the Ruhr area of Germany showing the Rhine and the town of Wesel.
Source Wikipedia. Copyright free

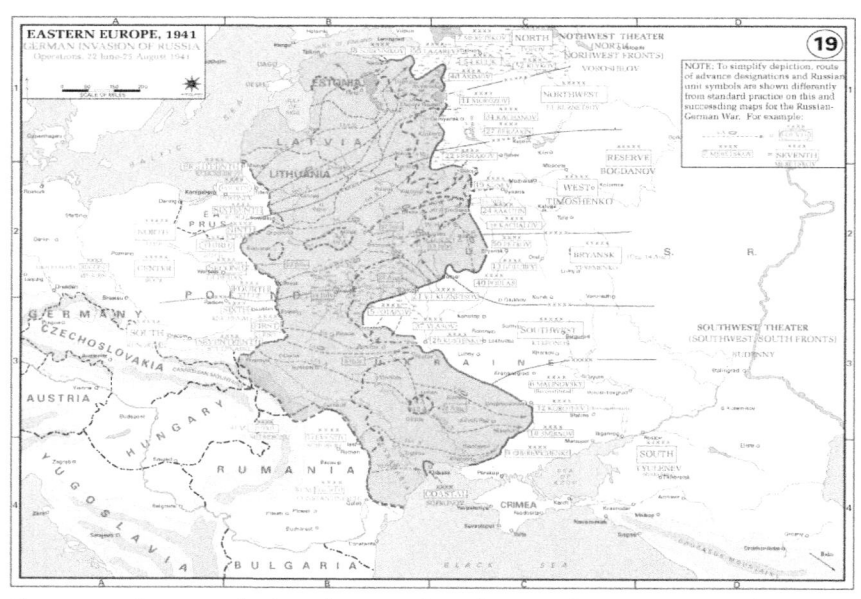

German advances during the opening phases of Operation Barbarossa, August 1941.
Source: Wikepedia Copyright free.

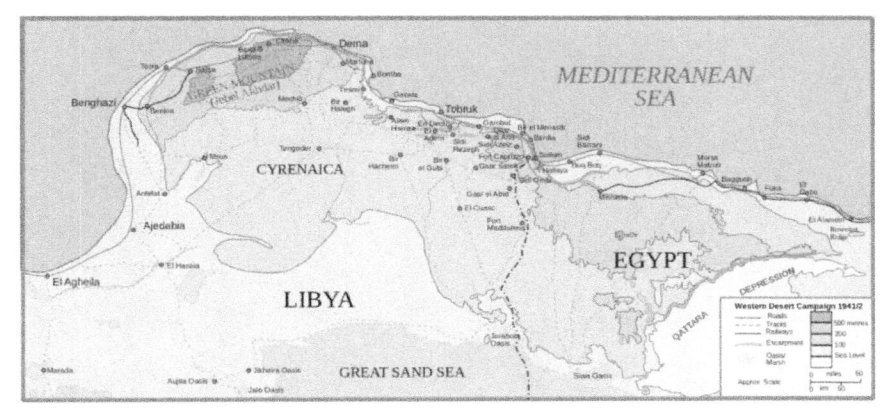

The Western Desert Campaign. 1941-42.
Source: Stephen Kirrage - Wikipedia. Copyright free.

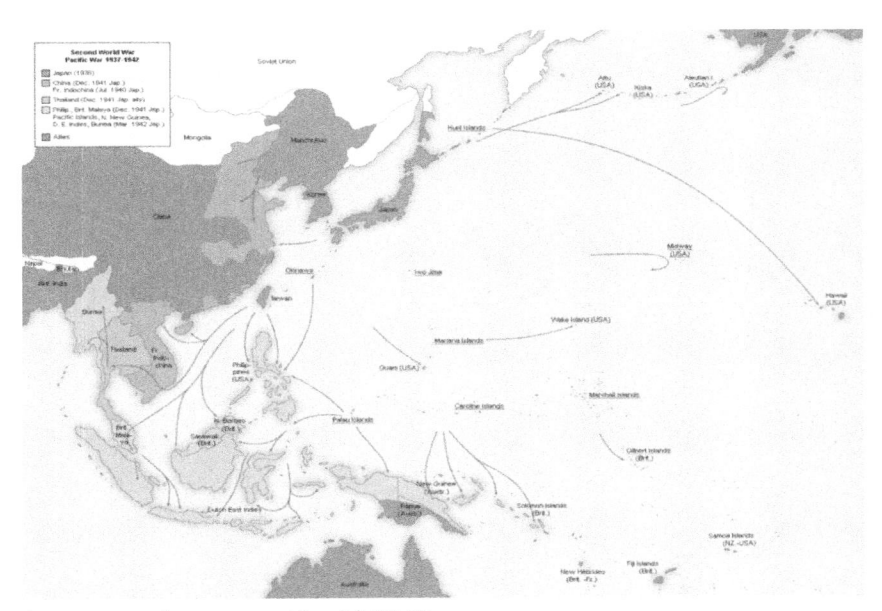

Japanese advances until mid-1942.
Source: Wikipedia. Copyright free.

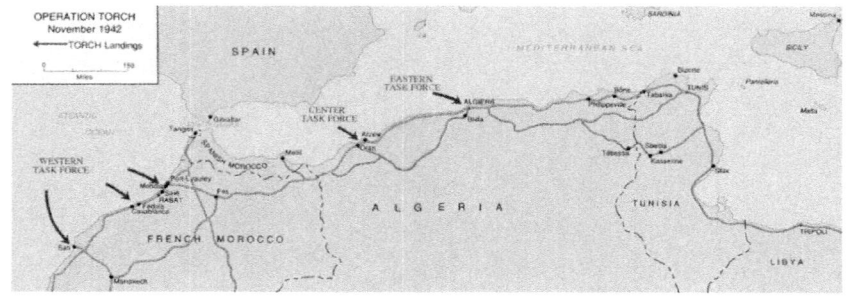

Operation Torch; November, 1942:
Source: Wikipedia. Copyright free.

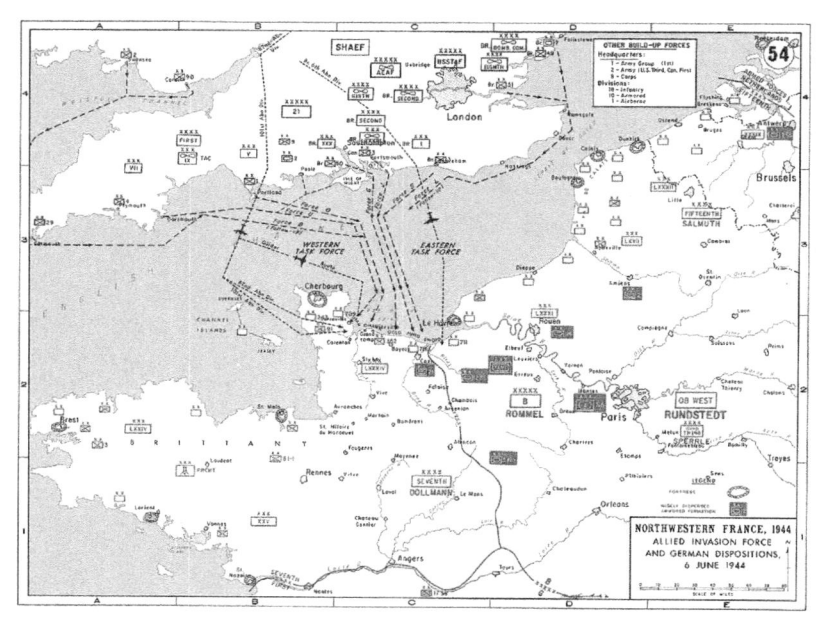

Allied invasion plans and German positions in Normandy.
Source: Wikipedia. Copyright free

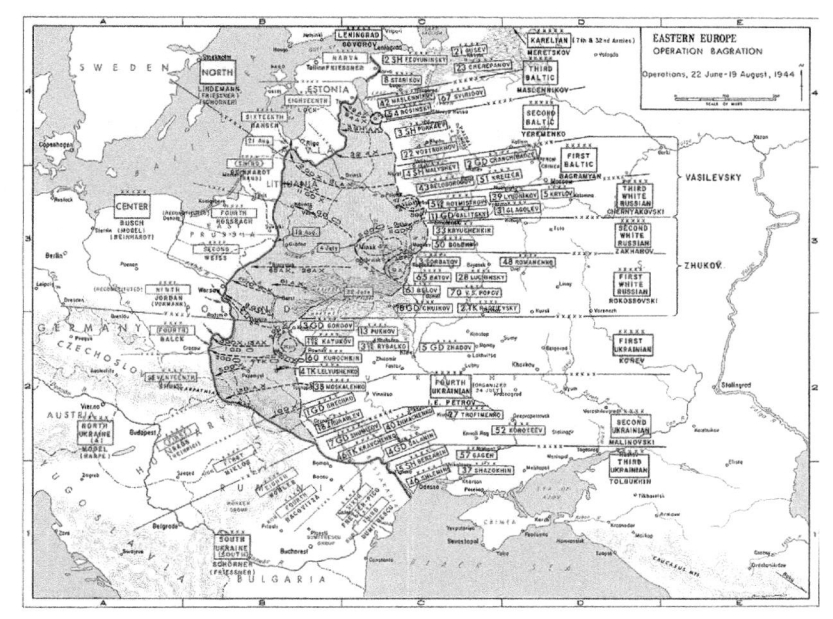

Army deployments for Operation Bagration.
Source: Wikipedia. Copyright free

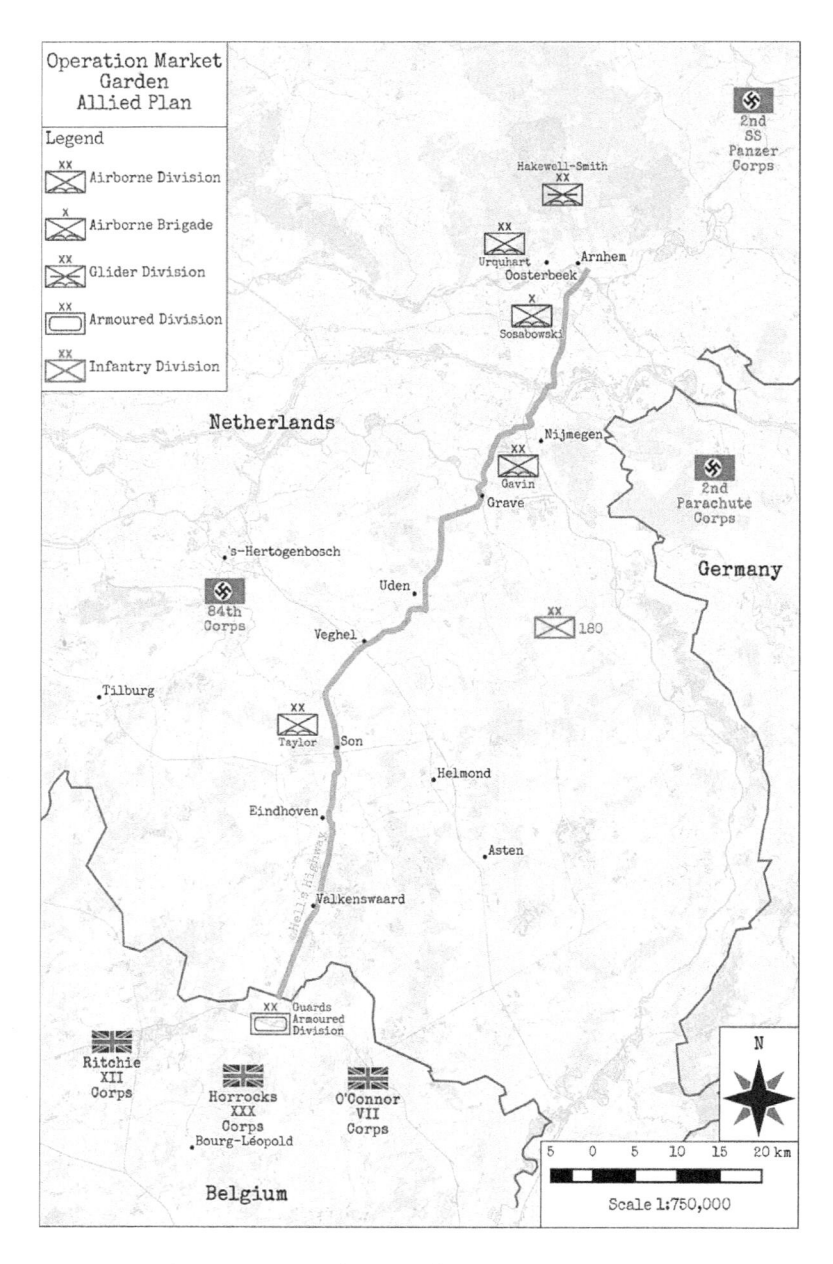

Operation Market Garden - The Allied Plan.
Source Duncan Jackson (via Wikipedia). Copyright free

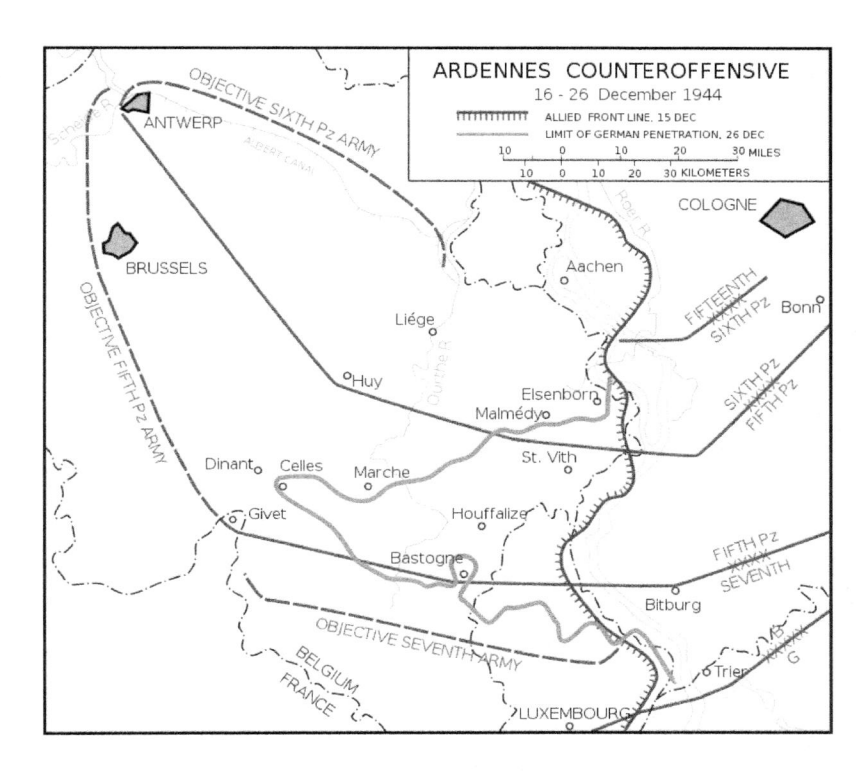

German counter attack through the Ardennes. December 1944.
The original objectives are shown by the red lines. The orange lines
indicate the actual advance.

Source: Wikepedia. Copyright free.

References, Sources and Further Reading.

Traditionally, the reference section of a history book is a neatly set out list of book titles, authors, publishers and publication dates.

Hopefully, as you have just read this book and perhaps even some of the other Layman's Guides that are available you have realised that these are not like most traditional history books. These days the way we access information has changed beyond measure from how we did it just a few years ago. It won't be long before reference and source pages such as this one will just have one word:

Google.

I may be being a bit facetious here, but you get my point.

I have used the internet extensively in the research and composition of this Layman's Guide. There are a plethora of websites that cover the history of the Second World War. (When I type in 'WW2' into Google I get over fifty million results!) Some of these pages are very good, some are not so good but if you take the time to filter out the rubbish bits there are some absolute gems out there.

Wikipedia is an obvious resource and with the Second World War there are thousands of different Wikipedia pages that concentrate on all aspects of the conflict. There is of course the usual caveat that goes along with all Wikipedia pages as sometimes they can mislead and misinform - I have tried to double check all information I have used from this site with other resources. They are good for maps though!

Many of the other 'usual web suspects' have also helped me with this book: The History Learning site (www.historylearningsite.co.uk) is a great resource and if you can navigate your way through the maze of First World War content which is understandably dominating the BBC's website at the moment, you can find some great stuff on the Second World War there too: www.bbc.co.uk/history/worldwars/wwtwo/ If forums are more your thing then may I recommend WW2 Talk (www.WW2talk.com) There are many knowledgeable chaps that hang out on this forum and they are all more than willing to help you out with any questions.

Print wise the list of books I have used to help put this Layman's Guide is long. Very long. Readers who want to go and learn more about the Second World War in general or dive deep into a specific theatre or battle are spoilt for choice. Currently on Amazon UK there are almost 40,000 books shown when you type in 'WW2' - so, where to start? Let me start with the epics. The big hitters are all there lining up to take your money in exchange for monumental works full of impressive academic research and minute detail. Anthony Beevor has his impressive *The Second World War* (W&N, 2014), Sir Max Hastings has his equally mammoth *All Hell Let Loose* (Harper Press, 2012) and Sir Martin Gilbert's *The Second World War* (Phoenix, 2009) is eyewatering in its completeness. If you have the stamina and the IQ to wade through any of these bohemoths, do it - you won't regret it.

Not content with churning out monsters on the overall conflict, these three heavyweight historians have also put together massive works on many of the separate battles of theatres of the war: Hastings has an impressive portfolio of work, some of his best include *Armageddon: The Battle for Germany 1944-45* (Pan, 2015) *Nemesis: The Battle for Japan, 1944--45* (Harper Perennial, 2008) and *Bomber Command* (Pan, 2010) which complements Richard Overy's brilliant *The Bombing War: Europe 1939-1945* (Penguin, 2014) perfectly.

For Operation Barbarossa and the subsequent fighting on the Eastern Front I relied heavily on *Barbarossa: The Russian-German Conflict, 1941-45* (Weidenfeld & Nicolson; New Ed, 2012) by Alan Clark as well as Robert Kershaw's *War Without Garlands: Operation Barbarossa 1941-42*

(Ian Allen, 2011). Tanks feature heavily on the Eastern Front and Robert Forczyk's *Tank Warfare on the Eastern Front 1941-1942* (Pen & Sword Military, 2014) was invaluable. Talking of tanks, Lloyd Clarke's *Kursk: The Greatest Battle* is a must read if you want to know the ins and outs of the biggest tank battle of the war. As well as these beauties, Anthony Beevor gets in on the Eastern Front act with the monumental *Stalingrad* (Penguin, 2007).

For D-Day I have relied on some of the biggest names in history. Stephen E. Ambrose is the self-professed king of D-Day and I have used *Pegasus Bridge* (Pocket Books, 2002) and *D-Day* (Simon & Shuster, 1994). Ambrose is ably helped by Sir Max Hastings with his revered *Overlord: D-Day and the Battle for Normandy 1944* (Pan Military Classics, 2010) and Anthony Beevor, who's mammoth *D-Day: The Battle for Normandy* (Viking, 2009) is not for the faint hearted but does contain some golden snippets that make it all worthwhile.

The war in Africa and Italy I can recommend *Destiny in the Desert* (Profile Books, 2012) by Jonathan Dimbleby as a very good read and also *Alamein* (Aurum Press, 2003) by Stephen Bungay, but to my mind Alan Moorehead's *The Desert War* trilogy (Aurum Press, 2013) is probably the definitive account of this theatre.

If you type in 'Pearl Harbor' into Amazon you get over 10,000 listings in the book department. That is a lot of pages dedicated to one attack that lasted a matter of hours. Two of the best are *Day of Infamy* by Walter Lord (Hnery Holt and Co, 2001) and *Pearl Harbor: Hinge of War* (Endeavour Press, 2015) by Richard Freeman. Freeman has also written a couple of other books about the Pacific theatre which are worth a look: *Coral Sea 1942* (Endeavour Press, 2013) and *Midway: The Battle That Made the Modern World* (Endeavour Press, 2012) are both valid titles if you want more details on these particular sea battles. For a wider view of the Pacific War I found *The Pacific War* (William Morrow, 1982) by John Costello to be an oldie but a goodie.

For Arnhem I relied heavily on *Arnhem 1944: The Airborne Battle* (Pen and Sword, 2012) by Martin Middlebrook and for Operation Market Garden (the Battle of the Bulge) you cannot ignore *Ardennes 1944: Hitler's Last Gamble* by Anthony Beevor although it is a very detailed and a bit of a difficult read. Beevor also tackles the final battle for Berlin in *Berlin: The Downfall 1945* (Penguin, 2007) but he is run very close in epic-ness by our old friend Sir Max Hastings with *Armageddon: The Battle for Germany 1944-45* (Pan, 2015).

As well as thousands of general narratives, there are also many hundreds of first-hand accounts of the Second World War, covering every battle of every theatre of war. Some of my favourites and ones that I used in putting this book together include *Spitfire Pilot: A Personal Account of the Battle of Britain* by Flight Lieutenant David Crook DFC (Albion Press, 2015) and *First Light* (Penguin, 2003) by Geoffrey Wellum which is a truly incredible read. The *Forgotten Voices* series of books is a remarkable written testimony to the men and women who were involved in the war and I cannot recommend them highly enough. They are all published by Ebury Press.

From the other side of the wire, some of the best German accounts of the war include *The Last Panther* (Bayern Classic Publications, 2015) and *Tiger Tracks* (Bayern Classic Publications, 2015) both written by Panzer crewman Wolfgang Faust. *D DAY Through German Eyes* by Holger Eckhertz (DTZ History Publications, 2015) is a remarkable and important study of what it was like to be a German infantryman in the bunkers and gun emplacements along the Normandy coast. Albrecht Wacker's *Sniper on the East Front* (Pen & Sword, 2005) is brutal and often violent, but it does manage to paint an honest picture of what the war was like on the Russian front. From a Luftwaffe point of view *The First and the Last* (Stellar Editions, 2014) by Adolf Galland is an amazing story, as is *Stuka Pilot* (Black House Publishing Ltd, 2011) by Hans Ulrich Rudel.

Happy reading!

Did you like this 'Layman's Guide'?

I really hope you liked this Layman's Guide. If you did, please take the time to leave a review on your local Amazon site. Nice reviews mean the world to me. If you didn't like it or think I can improve, please drop me a line – you can contact me via my website - www.scottaddington.com - I welcome all feedback, the only way I will improve as a writer is to listen to readers.

You may also be interested in some of the other Layman's Guides I have written - all are available from Amazon sites worldwide:

WW1: A Layman's Guide

D-Day: A Layman's Guide

The Third Reich: A Layman's Guide

Waterloo: A Layman's Guide

Thanks once again!
Scott

www.scottaddington.com

Printed in Great Britain
by Amazon